PREFACE

Like its predecessors TC 6-71 (1988) and the first field manual-version of FM 6-71 (1994), this publication is intended for you, the combined arms brigade or battalion commander, and your staffs to help you synchronize fires with your scheme of maneuver. You know from experience that combat forces must be employed as part of the combined arms team. Maneuver and fires must be synchronized and orchestrated by the combined arms commander to realize the full potential of each arm and maximize the combat power of the combined arms team. The same applies in principle to firepower. Mortars, cannon and rocket artillery, naval gunfire, and air support on the lethal side, and intelligence and electronic warfare (IEW) and information operations (IO) systems on the non-lethal side, are various means of fire support. Each has its own advantages and disadvantages. Each provides a measure of capability the others lack: responsiveness, flexibility, and accuracy from mortars and artillery; precision and destructiveness from close air support; disruption of command and control and capability to exclude collateral damage from IEW and IO systems. Using all of these means in combination creates a synergistic effect - the whole system is far more effective than its parts. The proper application of fire support requires as much skill and orchestration from the combined arms commander as it does from the fire support coordinator (FSCOORD). This is what this publication is about, to help clarify the art of applying fire support at the right time and place on the battlefield.

The proponent for this publication is HQ TRADOC. Send comments and recommended changes on DA Form 2028 (Recommended Changes to Publications and Blank Forms) directly to:

Commandant
US Army Field Artillery School
ATTN: ATSF-FR
Fort Sill, OK 73503-5600
DSN 639-5644

Comments and recommended changes can also be emailed to the USAFAS doctrine point of contact for this manual through the doctrine homepage at URL: http://155.219.39.98/doctrine/wddfrm.htm

FM 3-09.31 (FM 6-71)
MCRP 3-16C
1 OCTOBER 2002

By Order of the Secretary of the Army:

ERIC K. SHINSEKI
General, United States Army
Chief of Staff

Official:

Administrative Assistant to
the
Secretary of the Army
0224803

DISTRIBUTION: *Active Army, Army National Guard, and U.S. Army Reserve*: To be distributed in accordance with the initial distribution number, 114332, requirements for FM 3-09.31.

By direction of the Commandant of the Marine Corps

EDWARD HANLON JR.
Lieutenant General, U. S. Marine Corps
Marine Corps Combat Development
Command

Chapter 1

SYNCHRONIZATION

"There is still a tendency in each separate unit...to be a one- handed puncher. By that I mean that the rifleman wants to shoot, the tanker to charge, the artilleryman to fire...That is not the way to win battles. If the band played a piece first with the piccolo, then with the brass horn, then with the clarinet, and then with the trumpet, there would be a hell of a lot of noise but no music. To get the harmony in music each instrument must support the others. To get harmony in battle, each weapon must support the other. Team play wins. You musicians of Mars must not wait for the band leader to signal you...You must each of your own volition see to it that you come into this concert at the proper place and at the proper time..."

General George S. Patton, Jr., 8 July 1941, address to the men of the 2nd Armored Division, The Patton Papers, Vol. II, 1974

1-1. Synchronization is the arrangement of military actions in time, space and purpose to produce maximum relative combat power at a decisive place and time. Combined arms operations are the synchronized and simultaneous application of several arms, such as infantry, armor, aviation, artillery, engineer, intelligence, and air defense to achieve greater effects on the enemy than that achieved if each arm were used against the enemy in sequence or against separate objectives. The challenge to the combined arms commander is to achieve synchronization. While success in any battle, engagement, or operation is never guaranteed, its achievement is much more likely for the commander who can synchronize military actions.

1-2. The range of operations for which the combined arms commander must be able to synchronize military actions is broad. While primarily concentrating on offensive and defensive operations, he must also be able to synchronize his unit's activities during stability and support operations (SASO) when given those missions. In Chapter 2 this manual will address synchronization by defining important responsibilities for commanders and staff members of maneuver brigades and battalions.

1-3. FM 3-100.40 (100-40), *Tactics*, is the basic doctrinal reference for tactics. Knowledge of its contents is assumed for maneuver commanders. Similarly, armor and mechanized commanders delineate their tactics, techniques, and procedures (TTP) in the FM 71-series, infantry in the FM 7-series and aviation in the FM 1-series. Combined arms commanders must *insist* that their FSCOORDs and FSOs understand the maneuver TTP of these manuals - fire supporters must take it upon themselves to become as well versed as possible in maneuver TTP. Conversely, FSCOORDs and FSOs should *recommend* that their supported commander become familiar with the TTP of this manual and with the respective FM 3-09-series fire support TTP manual for their level of command. In Chapter 3, this manual addresses synchronization within a framework of the tactics of fire support by providing considerations for the commander during offensive, defensive, stability, and support operations. These considerations should be used to ensure the major planning and executing *fundamentals* of fire support are recognized and their utilization thought out as a concept of the operation is formulated.

1-4. In Chapter 4, this manual approaches synchronization through a discussion of the techniques and procedures for planning, preparing for and executing an operation where maneuver and fire support decisions are integrated throughout.

1-5. Fire support plans that are not integrated with maneuver plans result in unsuccessful fires in support of the operation. Integrating fire support leads to synchronization. It requires the commander and his staff to think both maneuver *and* fires at each step of the military decision making process (MDMP). Conversely, it should also cause commanders and staff to think both fires and maneuver throughout the targeting process. At brigade and battalion, the targeting process can be subsumed within the MDMP and requires no more people, equipment or time than what is used already in the MDMP. The MDMP and targeting process requires the same people: the battle staff. Targeting merely requires each member of the battle staff to provide more specific information and clearer focus at each step of the MDMP.

Key Terms and Definitions

1-6. Fire Planning. Fire planning is a continuous process, usually top-down driven or initiated, of planning and coordinating fire support requirements. Central to the process is the development and execution of essential fire support tasks (EFSTs). Conceptually, a fire plan is the logical sequence of executing EFSTs to support the concept of operation.

1-7. Targeting. Targeting is the process of selecting targets and matching the response to them, taking account of operational requirements and capabilities. It is a sub-process within the fire planning process specifically designed to manage only the DECIDE, DETECT, DELIVER and ASSESS (D3A) functions. Targeting occurs *within* the MDMP when the battle staff is developing an operations order (OPORD) (in this respect overlaying directly over many fire planning process functions) and occurs *outside* of the MDMP once the plan is completed (in this respect validating previous D3A decisions while planning for future D3A decisions).

1-8. Essential Fire Support Task. A task for fire support to accomplish that is required to support a combined arms operation. Failure to achieve an EFST may require the commander to alter his tactical or operational plan. A fully developed EFST has a task, purpose, method, and effects.

> **TASK**: Describes the targeting objective that fires must achieve against a specific enemy formation's function or capability. These formations are high-payoff

targets (HPTs) or contain one or more HPTs. TASK is normally expressed in terms of objective, formation, and function.

- Objective. Targeting objectives such as disrupt, delay, limit or destroy (per FM 6-20-10). Other terms can be used *as long as you and the FSCOORD share the same understanding of those terms.*
- Formation. A specific element or sub-element of the enemy. Can specify a specific vehicle type or target category as long as the mutual meaning (between maneuver commander and FSCOORD/FSO is clear).
- Function. A capability of the formation that is needed for it (the enemy formation) to achieve its primary task and purpose.

PURPOSE: Describes the maneuver or operational purpose for the task. Normally described *in terms of the maneuver purpose.* This should identify as specifically as possible the friendly maneuver formation that will benefit from the targeting objective and describe in space and time what the objective will accomplish.

METHOD: Describes *how* the task and purpose will be achieved. It ties the detect function to the deliver function in time and space and describes how to accomplish the task. Normally described in terms of priority, allocation and restriction. It is from the method of an EFST that subordinate units, including field artillery and target acquisition, get (some) of their essential tasks [essential field artillery tasks (EFAT) for artillery units].

- Priority. For detection assets, it assigns priorities for named area of interest (NAIs), target area of interest (TAIs), engagement areas (EAs), and/or HPTs to find. For deliver assets, it assigns the priority of which HPT that system will primarily be used against.
- Allocation. For both detection and deliver assets, it describes the allocation of assets to accomplish the EFST.
- Restriction. Describes constraints - either requirements to do something; or prohibition on action. Normal considerations include ammunition restrictions and fire support coordinating measures.

EFFECTS: Quantifying the successful accomplishment of the task - provides a guide to determine when we are done with the task. One measure of effects is to determine if the purpose was met. If multiple delivery assets are involved, it helps clarify what each must accomplish. Effects determination also provide the basis for the assess function of targeting and contribute to the decision of whether to re-attack the target.

1-9. Essential Field Artillery Task (EFAT). A task for the field artillery that must be accomplished to achieve an EFST. Is called an EFAT. A fully developed EFAT has a task, purpose, method, and effects. The task describes the effects of fires against a specific enemy formation(s) (effects of fires = suppress, neutralize, destroy, screen, or obscure). (**Note:** Fire family of scatterable mines/suppression of enemy air defense (FASCAM/SEAD) are special cases.) The **purpose** is a summary of the task and purpose from the EFST. The method describes how the task will be accomplished by assigning responsibilities to the FA batteries, survey and battalion tactical operations center (BN TOC). Typically the **method** is described by covering three categories: priority, allocation, and restrictions.

Priority provides the batteries with priority of fires (POF) and priority of survey. *Allocations* include movement triggers, routes, position areas, azimuths of fire, targets [priority and final protective fires (FPFs)], and radar zones. *Restrictions* cover fire support coordinating measure (FSCMs) and survivability movement criteria. **Effects** are a quantification of the FA task and positioning of FA units.

1-10. Concept of Fires. The logical sequence of EFSTs that integrated with the scheme of maneuver will accomplish the mission and achieve the commander's intent. Allocates in broad terms the fire support assets to achieve the EFSTs. The concept of fires is the basis of the fires paragraph.

1-11. Scheme of Fires. The detailed, logical sequence of targets and fire support events to find and attack the HPTs. It details how we expect to execute the fire support plan in accordance with the time and space of the battlefield to accomplish the commander's essential fire support tasks. The products of the fire support (FS) annex: fire support execution matrix (FSEM), target list/overlay, and/or a modified target synchronization matrix (TSM) articulate the scheme of fires.

Chapter 2

FIRE SUPPORT RESPONSIBILITIES

"Our goal must be to enable combined arms commanders to fight fire support systems with the same skill and vigor with which they employ direct fire systems."

MG Fred F. Marty, Chief
of Field Artillery, June 1992

2-1. You have a FSCOORD at each echelon of command from company through brigade. At company and battalion levels, he is the fire support officer (FSO). At brigade level, the direct support (DS) battalion commander is the FSCOORD; his full-time assistant is the brigade FSO. The FSCOORD's and FSO's first obligation is to enable combined arms commanders to synchronize fires with maneuver. They accomplish this by understanding your intent, translating your guidance into EFSTs, advising you and your staff on the proper employment of fire support means and actively managing the execution of the fire support plan. Each time you sit down with your S3 to discuss current or future plans, concepts or courses of action, your FSCOORD or FSO should be there. While the FSCOORD and FSO are the primary fire support coordinators, virtually everyone on a brigade or battalion staff has a role in the synchronization challenge, as described in the remainder of this chapter.

MANEUVER COMMANDER

2-2. Major responsibilities for fire support include:

- *Synchronize* fire support with the scheme of maneuver.
- Ensure the FSCOORD and FSO understand your *fire support guidance*. Use doctrinal terms per <u>FM 101-5-1</u>, *Operational Terms and Graphics*, and <u>FM 3-100.40</u> or more descriptive language, but state the TASK(s) and PURPOSE(s) in no uncertain terms. Focus on the what, where, when (and for how long) and why - your FSCOORD/FSO will recommend the how.
- Ensure your staff integrates reconnaissance and surveillance (R&S), maneuver, fires (including offensive IO and other non-lethal means if applicable), Army airspace command and control (A2C2), and obstacles. Have someone responsible for *overlaying the overlays* - whether analog or electronic.
- Approve the fires paragraph, high-payoff target list (HPTL), attack guidance matrix (AGM), target selection standards (TSS), or a TSM that combines the preceding three, the EFST, and their logical execution sequence.
- Approve FSCMs.
- Clear fires in zone. Normally this is managed at the TOC with the FSO or FS Plans Officer leading the TOC and subordinate units through a clearance of fire battle drill. (More on clearance of fires in <u>Chapter 4</u>).

- Train company and team commanders to know, understand and execute targets in their zone. Train the staff and brigade reconnaissance troop (BRT) commander on proper tactical employment of the Striker platoon.

MANEUVER EXECUTIVE OFFICER (XO)

2-3. Major responsibilities for fire support include:

- Integrate the targeting process into the MDMP and normal brigade/battalion battle rhythm.
- Supervises the DECIDE function of targeting. (Target meetings are key to success. More on targeting meetings in Chapter 4)

MANEUVER S3

2-4. Major responsibilities for fire support include:

- In the absence of the XO, integrate targeting into the MDMP and conduct targeting meetings.
- Based on the FSO's recommendation, integrate all fire support assets into the concept of the operation.
- Select, with the commander, combined arms engagement areas to kill the enemy.
- Develop the synchronization matrix that includes fire support.
- Develop a decision support template (DST) with input from the FSO.
- Integrate fire support actions and the execution of EFSTs into the combined arms rehearsal.
- Approve positioning of field artillery and other fire support assets.
- With input from the staff, especially the S2 and FSO, decide the HPTs that will be presented to the commander for approval.

MANEUVER S2

2-5. Major responsibilities for fire support include:

- Participate in the targeting process. Develop high-value targets (HVTs). Recommend HPTs. Provide input to the FSO on TSS. Supervises execution of the DETECT and ASSESS functions of targeting.
- Develop an R&S plan with input from the S3, FSO, Engineer and Air Defence Artillery liaison officer (ADA LNO) that synchronizes targeting requirements with collection assets.
- In conjunction with the staff, especially the FSO and targeting officer, develop targets.

TTP TIP

> Give all battle staff officers/NCOs the responsibility of assisting the S2 with intelligence preparation of the battlefield (IPB). At a minimum, each can contribute in refining situation templates for high-value targets within their battlefield operating system (BOS). The S2 will benefit from collective staff knowledge on the enemy; the staff will benefit from greater insights on the effects of IPB on their friendly BOS systems.

- Brief analysis and control element (ACE) sections on HPTL, TSS and AGM.
- Disseminate HPT related information and intelligence to FS immediately.

BRIGADE/BATTALION ENGINEER

2-6. Major responsibilities for fire support include:

- Determine if the maneuver commander plans to provide survivability positions for FA assets and what the priority is for those positions.
- Plan for scatterable mines (SCATMINE) - including those FA-delivered. Coordinate with the S3, S2 and FSO for emplacement. Track the amount of available FA SCATMINE
- Coordinate fire support coverage of designated mine fields and other obstacles. Ensure that the indirect fire plan is synchronized with the obstacle plan.
- Determine SCATMINE safety box and disseminate the scatterable mine report.
- Ensure FA SCATMINE is deconflicted in terms of FA mission priorities and emplacement time requirements. Report emplacement of FA-delivered SCATMINE.
- In conjunction with the S2 and FSO continuously adjust target locations as planned locations become emplaced obstacles.

BRIGADE/BATTALION CHEMICAL OFFICER

2-7. Major responsibility for fire support is:

- Recommend where chemical smoke can be used to augment or be used in lieu of artillery smoke

AIR LIAISON OFFICER (ALO)/TACP

2-9. Major responsibilities for fire support include:

- Supervise the TACP.
- Coordinate and monitor requests for close air support (CAS) and air interdiction. Ensure requests are timely to be included in air tasking order (ATO) cycle requirements.
- Keep the S3 and FSO informed of the current status of available air support.

- TACPs assist in the integration and synchronization of air support, coordination of preplanned and immediate air requests, and in the coordination of A2C2 issues.
- Battalion TACPs are responsible for terminal attack control.

FSCOORD/DS BATTALION COMMANDER

2-10. Major responsibilities for fire support include:

- Plans and coordinates fire support for the maneuver brigade. Is the principal advisor on fire support matters to the brigade commander. Collocate with the brigade commander as necessary, but normally during mission execution.
- Commands the unit providing primary fire support to the force.
- Participates as feasible with the brigade orders group and during targeting meetings. Assists in the synchronization of fires and maneuver.
- Provides accurate, timely and effective FA fires.
- Approves the DS battalion field artillery support plan (FASP). Ensures the plan provides executing instructions for assigned EFATs. As the DS battalion commander, provides an intent statement (1st subparagraph of paragraph 3 of the FASP) for his field artillery staff, subordinate commander's and soldiers.

BRIGADE FSO

2-11. Major responsibilities for fire support include:

- Assists in the planning and coordination of fire support for the maneuver brigade. In the FSCOORD's absence is the principal advisor on fire support matters (assets, capabilities, limitations, and missions) to the brigade commander and his staff.
- Assists in the synchronization of fires and maneuver.
- Coordinates the DELIVER function of targeting. Directs the attack of targets by fires in accordance with (IAW) the priorities and effects established by the maneuver commander.
- Keeps the maneuver commander, FSCOORD and staff informed of the current status, location, and activity of all fire support assets.
- In conjunction with the targeting officer and DS battalion S2, keeps the maneuver S2 informed of enemy indirect fire capabilities and limitations.
- Participate in the MDMP and targeting process, keeping the DS battalion S3 informed throughout. Develop for approval: the fire support plan with EFSTs and supporting products (HPTL, AGM, TSS, TSM, and FSEM). Disseminate approved plans and products to the DS artillery battalion, battalion FSOs, division FSE, and div arty.
- Ensures battalion FSOs are aware of assigned EFSTs and are refining targets IAW top-down fire planning. Produces the brigade target list.
- Acts upon and coordinates requests for fire support from battalion FSOs. Continually assess fire support asset availability and recommends priorities and allocation of fire support.

- Resolves duplication on planned target lists.
- Manages the clearance of fire battle drill within the TOC.
- Recommends FSCMs.
- Assists the S3 in terrain management for fire support assets.
- Coordinates with the ALO and S3 Air for use of CAS and with the S3 Air for A2C2 actions.
- Coordinates with the IEW, IO,civil affairs (CA), psychological operations (PSYOP) and other non-lethal representatives as appropriate for the non-lethal attack of targets and integration of IO into the concept of the operation.
- Coordinates with the engineer representative to plan fires to support mobility and countermobility operations.
- During the MDMP and targeting meetings, recommends with assistance from the S2 and S3, what targets to attack, when, where, and with what assets (lethal/non-lethal).

1-3. <u>FM 3-100.40</u> (100-40), *Tactics*, is the basic doctrinal reference

- Anticipates changes during mission execution and recommends and coordinates revisions to the fire support plan.
- Coordinates with the div arty, maneuver S2, targeting officer, battalion FSOs and DS battalion S3 and S2, to plan for the employment of Firefinder radars and the establishment and managing of radar zones.
- Coordinates with the ALO on enemy air defense capabilities and employment plans to suppress or destroy enemy air defense as necessary during CAS and Army aviation employment.
- Participates in combined arms rehearsals and conduct fire support rehearsals.
- Assists the maneuver S3 in planning combat observation/lasing team (COLT) and Striker employment to ensure they are integrated into the overall R&S plan.

BRIGADE FIRE SUPPORT PLANS OFFICER

2-12. Major responsibilities for fire support include:

- Assists the brigade FSO perform his duties and acts as the FSO in his absence.
- See responsibilities of FSO above.

TARGETING OFFICER

2-13. Major responsibilities for fire support include:

- Coordinate with the maneuver S2 to facilitate the rapid attack of HPTs.
- Pass important intelligence to the FSO and units providing fire support to the force.
- Assist the brigade S2 with the R&S plan by providing input on radar zones and search sectors.
- Manage changes to radar zones. Coordinate with all affected elements.

- Assist in the development of targeting products.
- Coordinates with the brigade S2 and FSO, to manage the detect, deliver, and assess functions on brigade HPTs.

DS BATTALION S3

2-14. Major responsibilities for fire support include:

- IAW the brigade OPORD, div arty FASP and guidance received from the DS battalion commander, plans for the accomplishment of EFATs.
- Coordinates positioning of FA assets with the brigade S3 through the FSO, to include positions for reinforcing FA elements.
- Participates as feasible in the brigade MDMP and combined arms rehearsals.

TTP TIP

When possible, have the DS battalion S3 at the maneuver TOC through as much of the MDMP as he can afford. The field artillery piece of synchronization will be better managed and parallel planning will be enhanced - he just has to maintain constant communications with his TOC.

BATTALION FSO

2-15. Major responsibilities for fire support include:

- The fire support coordinator for the maneuver battalion commander. His primary advisor on all matters pertaining to fire support.
- Perform the same or similar duties for the battalion as the brigade FSO does for brigade.
- Coordinate with the S2 and S3, to assist in the development of the battalion observation plan. Plans for and supervises the execution of assigned and developed EFSTs.
- Participate in brigade and battalion combined-arms and fire support rehearsals.
- Recommends to the maneuver battalion commander how to best employ and control fire support teams (FISTs). Options include centralized control of a *pool* of FISTs to execute brigade and battalion EFSTs; decentralized control down to company level to execute brigade, battalion and company EFSTs; or, a combination of the two.
- Recommends to the S3 battalion mortar employment and usage considerations.
- Ensure that the targets received on the brigade target list are refined as necessary and sent back to the brigade FSO.

COMPANY COMMANDER

2-16. Major responsibilities for fire support include:

- Ensures assigned targets are refined, observed, rehearsed and fired in according to the scheme of fires.
- Positions fire support personnel where they can best execute EFSTs.
- Ensures the company FSO participates in all combined arms and fire support rehearsals.

COMPANY FSO

2-17. Major responsibilities for fire support include:

- The fire support coordinator for the maneuver company commander. His primary advisor on all matters pertaining to fire support.
- Assists the company commander in planing for and supervising the execution of assigned and developed EFSTs.
- Refines brigade and battalion targets assigned to the company.
- Participates in combined arms (brigade through company) and fire support rehearsals.

COLT TEAM CHIEF and STRIKER PLATOON LEADER

2-18. Major responsibilities for fire support include:

- Execute brigade EFSTs.
- Initiate fires on targets within TAI, EAs, or trigger points.
- IAW with information received from brigade reconnaissance observation of NAIs, act as the brigade commander's *killer* of targets outside of battalion direct fire/scout range.

INTELLIGENCE AND ELECTRONIC WARFARE STAFF OFFICER

2-19. Major responsibilities for fire support include:

- Coordinate with FSCOORD
- Advise the commander and staff on the electronic attack of HPTs.
- Advise the commander and staff of possible IEW actions to help achieve non-lethal targeting guidance/desired effects during the MDMP and targeting meetings.
- Conduct frequency deconfliction.
- Advise the commander on IEW as it pertains to information operations.

STAFF JUDGE ADVOCATE

2-20. Major responsibilities for fire support include:

- Advise the commander and staff on the legal ramifications of the attack of each HPT.

- Provide rules of engagement (ROE) advice and expertise during planning and execution.

PSYOP REPRESENTATIVE

2-21. Major responsibilities for fire support include:

- Keep the commander and staff informed of psychological operations or events that could impact the unit.
- Advise the commander and staff on possible psychological operations including PSYACTS to help achieve non-lethal targeting guidance/desired effects during the MDMP and targeting meetings.

CIVIL AFFAIRS REPRESENTATIVE

2-22. Major responsibilities for fire support include:

- Keep the commander and staff informed of civilian activities that could impact the unit.
- Advise the commander and staff on possible civil affair operations to help achieve (targeting) guidance during the MDMP and targeting meetings.

INFORMATION OPERATIONS (IO) COORDINATOR

2-23. Major responsibilities for fire support include:

- Keep the commander and staff informed of all IO that could impact the unit.
- Advise the commander and staff on possible IO actions to help achieve non-lethal targeting guidance during the MDMP and targeting meetings.

MILITARY INTELLIGENCE (MI) COMPANY COMMANDER

2-24. Major responsibilities for fire support include:

- Keeps staff informed on status of organic and attached collection and electronic attack assets.
- Ensure assigned detect, deliver (if applicable), and assess tasks are planned and prepared for and executed IAW the concept of the operation, R&S plan, and target synchronization matrix (if applicable).
- Coordinate the use of unmanned aerial vehicle (UAVs) and other collection assets to assist in target acquisition and battle damage assessment (BDA).
- Participate in the MDMP process.

AVIATION LNO

2-25. Major responsibilities for fire support include:

- Advise the commander and staff on the use of attached/operational control (OPCON) aviation assets.
- Assist in A2C2 management.
- Exchange targeting information with parent headquarters during the MDMP and immediately following targeting meetings.
- Participate in the MDMP process.

AIR DEFENSE ARTILLERY LNO

2-26. Major responsibilities for fire support include:

- Assist in A2C2 management.
- Provide SME advice on enemy ADA capabilities during SEAD operations.
- Coordinate with the S3 Air, ALO and ALO/TACP on airspace control measures.

Chapter 3

THE TACTICS OF FIRE SUPPORT

"No one starts a war - or rather, no one in his senses ought to do so - **without first being clear** *in his mind* **what he intends to achieve** *by that war and* **how he intends to conduct it**. *The former is its political purpose; the later its operational objective. This is the governing principle which will set its course,* **prescribe the scale of means and effort which is required,** *and make its influence felt throughout down to the* **smallest operational detail**.*" (emphasis added)*

> Field Marshall Carl von Clausewitz,
> On War, viii, 1832,
> tr. Howard and Paret

3-1. The ideas set forth by Carl von Clausewitz over 150 years ago on the nature of war still have tactical applicability today. As a unit prepares for an operation and the staff conducts the MDMP, the commander visualizes the purpose, objective and key tasks and expresses them as his intent. Additionally, he will give planning guidance to his staff to assist in course of action (COA) development. This chapter provides fire support considerations for various types of operations. Gaining an appreciation of how to apply fire support in offensive, defensive, stability and support operations, as well as during military operations on urban terrain (MOUT), breaching, passages of lines, and airborne and air assault operations, will help you develop your guidance for fire support and key you in on the type of information the FSCOORD / FSO should provide.

OFFENSIVE OPERATIONS

3-2. Fire support in offensive operations is characterized by centralized planning with decentralized execution. Planning factors, such as EFSTs, on order missions, priorities of fire, FSCMs, and so forth, must be developed within a flexible framework to allow changes to be made and efficiently disseminated, understood, and implemented. Before you issue your planning guidance, and as part of visualizing your decisive point(s), determine how fires will set the conditions for actions at the decisive point(s)/objective(s) and/or how they will augment your actions at those decisive points/objectives.

TTP TIP

Place FSCMs, especially the coordinated fire line (CFL) if established, where they make tactical (IAW a mission, enemy, terrain and weather, troops, time available, and civil considerations (METT-TC) analysis) sense and aid in facilitating the attack of targets (permissive) or preventing fratricide (restrictive) For example, always using phase lines as CFLs may

---

> fail to account for the enemy consideration of METT-TC for FSCM establishment and can hamper, rather than assist, the rapid attack of targets of opportunity.

Movement to Contact

3-3. Consider placing a battery with the advance guard in a brigade movement to contact (MTC) or battalion mortars with the advance guard in a task force MTC to provide immediately responsive fires. Paladin units are ideally suited for supporting this operation because of their fast emplacements and on-board computing capability. (see FM 3-09.21, *Training, Tactics, and Procedures for the Field Artillery Battalion* (FM 6-20-1) for dedicated battery considerations.)

3-4. Once contact is made, the brigade (FSCOORD's recommendation; your decision) must be prepared to shift priority of fires to the unit in contact and control of all available fires to the observer who is in the best position to control fires against the enemy.

3-5. If intelligence supported, have fires planned on reserves and uncommitted forces to facilitate freedom of action once contact is made. Have fires planned along the axis of advance to assist in dealing with contingencies. Additionally, plan fires on possible counterattack avenues of approach against forces other than reserves and uncommitted units that may influence the operation. Likely support by fire positions should be covered with an on-call critical friendly zone (CFZ). Have the staff consider fire support to security and reconnaissance forces. Consider consolidating FIST assets. Is it necessary for the trail battalion or companies to retain their FISTs when those personnel could be executing brigade EFSTs or augmenting the lead battalion/company?

3-6. The proper synchronization of maneuver with fires demands that rehearsals consider the movement of fire support assets (who, when, where, how) tied to flexible, yet known, triggers. Ensure the FSCOORD is maximizing the use of priority targets and that these targets are being put into effect and canceled based on the forward element's movement. Ensure the FSCOORD/FSO plans for possible breaching operations considering the S(uppress) and O(bscure) of suppress, obscure, secure, and reduce (SOSR).

Example EFST for a Movement to Contact.

> Task: Disrupt ability of enemy squads to withdraw once in contact.

> Purpose: To allow unit in contact to fire/ maneuver and destroy with direct fires.

> Method: Execute priority targets with mortars first, then artillery. One artillery target allocated to each task force (TF). COLTs priority is to locate elements of the regimental artillery group (RAG) for proactive counterfire.

Effects: Provide a sustained duration of suppressive fires that the enemy must risk maneuvering through in order to withdraw.

Hasty Attack

3-7. Depending on time available, fire support plans are generally more centralized and directive. Consider the use of quick fire planning techniques. In a quick fire plan, the respective FSO leads the targeting team to develop EFSTs using very specific guidance from the maneuver commander. Once the commander approves the EFSTs, mission-type orders are issued to the necessary detect an deliver asset to accomplish the purpose of the EFST. The plan is developed, disseminated and executed in a very short period of time. Brigade and battalion staffs should develop standing operating procedures (SOP) items that facilitate such fire planning under time constraints.

3-8. In all offensive actions, particularly this one and the movement to contact, because of an unclear enemy situation or lack of detailed planning time, the detect function will be the most difficult to execute. Give the R&S and observation plans your personal attention (if feasible).

3-9. Realize subordinate units will also have less time to plan for this type of operation. On the fire support side, this might mean the DS battalion S3 (and his S2 and fire direction officer (FDO)) as well as the battalion FSOs or FS noncommissioned officers (NCOs) should be at the brigade TOC while the plan is being developed (at least through COA decision).

3-10. If a hasty attack is being conducted from a transition out of a movement to contact, have clear triggers for command or support relationship changes (if any are planned). For example, a COLT or Striker team attached to the lead battalion reverts back to brigade control.

Deliberate Attack

3-11. There should be time to *overlay the overlays*. Has the S3 ensured that the R&S plan, scheme of maneuver, fire support plan, engineer plan, and others are all integrated with each other?

3-12. Use fires, both lethal and non-lethal, to set conditions for success at decisive points/objectives. Employ COLTs and Strikers to execute brigade EFSTs; some EFSTs will probably have to be executed by subordinate battalions. The top-down fire plan should appear to be one seamless scheme of fires. If CAS, attack aviation, and/or air assault operations are planned, include SEAD in all fire planning.

3-13. Ensure that the FSCOORD or FSO discuss with you and your staff the pros and cons of preparation fire before you issue planning guidance. This will become a significant EFST if a preparation is part of your concept of the operation. Establish a definite trigger, initiated by a maneuver force, for the lifting and/or shifting of fires; consider redundant signals and *rehearse them.*

3-14. Enforce target refinement cutoff times. Consider carefully the decisions you will have to make based on an assessment of executed fires (have the conditions been set?) - what redundant means have been planned?

3-15. Bypass criteria and engagement criteria (for example: "No FA fires on single moving vehicles") are very important for the FSCOORD so that he can not only tell his subordinates what threats they may face while moving to support you, but also help keep fires focused on EFSTs and HPTs. (There is more on attack guidance in Chapter 4). Bottom line: are fires supporting your concept throughout the area of operations (AO) for the duration of the mission? Has the FSCOORD adequately accounted for the movement of field artillery and other fire support assets as the attack progresses?

Example EFSTs for a Deliberate Attack.

> Task: Disrupt the enemy on objective from effectively engaging attacking forces with direct fires.

> Purpose: Allow infantry to close and engage the enemy with direct fires.

> Method: Echelon CAS, artillery and mortar suppressive fires across the objective. Priority of fires to TF 2-64, target AD0018, Bn 6 rounds (rds) with marking round and 2 sorties A-10 CAS. airspace coordination area (ACA) Blue in effect.

> Effects: CAS destroys 1 platoon; artillery and mortars provide continuous (sustained rate of fire) fires within 200 meters (m) of other 2 platoons until cease or shift fire is ordered.

> Task: Limit the enemy's ability to effectively observe the actions of the breach force and assault force vicinity the point of breach.

> Purpose: Allow breach force to reduce enemy obstacle and assault force to commence the assault to secure the far side.

> Method: Continuous artillery and/or mortar smoke screen between enemy within direct fire range of the point of signals that its objective is secure. breach and the obstacle. COLT initiates smoke then hands off to TF 2-64, target AD0008, 1000m smoke screen for 30 minutes. TF observers control mortar smoke.

> Effects: Effective smoke continues until assault force signal that its objective is secure.

> **TTP TIP**
>
> In breaching operations, suppression and obscuration fires will be planned. The key for effective FA support here is not just stating *how much* but *for how long.* Express your desired suppressive effects by clearly articulating duration or another observable end-state (or condition that has been met).

Exploitation and/or Pursuit

3-16. Use fires, both lethal and non-lethal to sustain your momentum. FA movement for this phase of the operation should be planned as part of the original order. Again, Paladin units are ideally suited for supporting these operations. Gauge your rate of advance based on FA movement. Consider using fires to suppress pockets of resistance to allow uninterrupted advance of maneuver units.

3-17. Plan fires to slow the enemy's withdrawal and to disrupt reinforcements. If SCATMINE are used, precise safety determination and dissemination are critical so that friendly momentum will not be lost. The management of FSCMs and radar zone changes will have to be executed quicker in these operations - your decision will be sought here.

DEFENSIVE OPERATIONS

3-18. Fire support in defensive actions is characterized by centralized planning with centralized execution. Planning factors, such as EFSTs, on order missions, priorities of fire, FSCMs, final protective fires, use of minimum safe distances, and risk estimate distances, to list the more common, must be developed to support a synchronized attack at the place and time you want to kill the enemy. Before you issue your planning guidance, and as part of visualizing your decisive point(s), determine how fires will set the conditions for actions at the decisive point (s) and/or how they will augment your actions at those decisive points. The combined use of obstacles and fires in the defense plays a larger role in the concept of the operation because of the importance of countermobility. However, all BOS must be synchronized as in the offense. Fires are planned, and EFSTs determined, as in the offense.

Area Defense

3-19. Initial priority of fires is normally allocated to (forward) security forces. If the enemy is attacking in echelons, isolate the first echelon by initially focusing fires on the follow-on echelon(s).

3-20. Consider counter-preparation fires to disrupt enemy preparatory fires. Planning considerations for this EFST are similar to a preparation in terms of ammunition consumption, counterfire, and assets required.

3-21. If the defense is planned as a phased operation (counter-reconnaissance, security zone, main battle, counterattack), EFSTs should be designated for each phase with triggers and dissemination instructions identified for when they change.

3-22. Specify engagement criteria for each phase of the defense. Single, lightly armored vehicles may be approved for FA attack during counter-reconnaissance operations but not during the main battle.

3-23. The FSCOORD should be coming to you asking for engineer assets to provide survivability positions for FA weapon and radar systems. This need will apply to the mortars at battalion level. As for FSCMs, you can place the CFL close to your forward elements (have a trigger planned to move it once security forces join the main battle area) to facilitate the rapid attack of targets.

Security Zone Considerations

3-24. The positioning of fire support assets for the defense has to include considerations for support of security zone actions. Augment the security zone with additional observers. This will depend on the number and location of EFSTs to be executed. Ensure the FSO has considered communications with security forces, especially battalion scouts and COLTs/Strikers if operating in your AO.

Main Battle Area Considerations

3-25. Ammunition expenditures are historically higher in the defense. Ensure the FSCOORD or FSO back-briefs you on the FA capability to execute EFATs and how loss of weapons and/or ammunition affects that capability.

3-26. If possible, tell the FSCOORD "...here is where I want every artillery piece in the brigade available to fire..." and indicating either an EA or TAI, specific time, a condition that presents itself, or a combination of these factors. Be as specific as possible in designating which obstacles will be covered with indirect fires. Your FSOs ought to recommend as part of a COA which, or how many, obstacles can be covered (you may have to prioritize). Providing redundant observers for EFSTs is relatively easier in the defense. Ensure the FSO does so in his observer plan.

3-27. A FPF is a special mission used only in defensive operations. The FSCOORD/FSO recommends who gets them; you approve them.

3-28. Have the S3, FSO, ALO/TACP, ADA LNO, and S3 Air ensure there is no conflict between ACA, air corridors and indirect fire positions.

TTP TIP

The maneuver commander, not the FSO, is responsible for executing

EFSTs from the OPORD. That responsibility includes ensuring the target is refined, observed, rehearsed and executed according to the scheme of fires. You can help ensure that your subordinate commanders understand this by including EFST responsibility in paragraph 3d of the OPORD (tasks to subordinate units). During rehearsals, have your *maneuver commanders* articulate their *fire support responsibilities*

Rear Area Considerations

3-29. The principles of FS planning and coordination in the rear areas do not differ significantly from those in the forward areas and apply to both the offense and defense. There is, however, a difference in the facilities available. Rear command post (CPs) have only limited manpower and limited communications facilities

3-30. Consider the use of attack helicopters and slower fixed-wing CAS because of their ability to actually observe the target and thus avoid nearby friendly elements. In fact, attack helicopters may be the most responsive and efficient means of providing FS to the rear area operations.

3-31. With few exceptions, indirect fire assets should not be employed against a Level I threat or against those Level II threat forces that can be defeated by base or base cluster units or by the reaction force. Level III threats have the size and combat power which could require the use of indirect fire assets.

3-32. The forces already on station are responsible for fighting the rear enemy initially. The immediate problem for rear operations is how to manipulate the limited resources, including FS, at the right time and place. Considerations that affect the application of FS for rear operations are as follows:

- The reduction of FS to the decisive or shaping operation.
- The suitability as determined by the overall tactical situation.
- The responsiveness of the available weapon systems.
- The precision and collateral damage effects of the weapon systems.
- The existence of communications nets to facilitate FS activities.
- The availability of observers to identify targets and adjust fires.

3-33. The applicable FSCMs for rear area operations will be restrictive measures [for example, no fire areas (NFAs), restrictive fire area (RFA)s and restrictive fire line (RFLs)]. The operations cell of the rear CP should establish them. The procedures for establishing FSCMs in the rear area must become part of the overall planning process. Forces employed to deal with a Level III force in the rear normally are given an AO. The establishment of a boundary within the rear and the possible addition of a task force FSO require close coordination with the rear CP. These measures should be reviewed routinely by higher headquarters (HQ); posted on rear CP operations maps; entered into the advanced field artillery tactical data system (AFATDS); and given to any supporting component forces and reaction forces.

3-34. The supporting FA must be positioned to support rear operations if assigned that EFAT. Since the rear area does not have a maneuver unit with FSO normally assigned to it, the headquarters and headquarters battery (HHB) battery commander (out of the DS battalion) often serves as an ad hoc rear area fire support officer. Positioning coordination with the rear CP operations cell of the base support battalion (BSB) or headquarters and headquarters company (HHC), depending on the level of command) is necessary to avoid fratricide of combat support (CS) and combat service support (CSS) units and destruction of critical supplies when FA and other FS means receive counterfire. This action also facilitates the ability of the rear CP to coordinate terrain management, movement control, and sustainment.

3-35. Potentially, all FS systems are available for deployment in rear area operations. Practically, some are more suitable and all depend on the factors of METT-TC.

Mobile Defense

3-36. If part of the striking force, retain your DS battalion - even prior to commitment. This simplifies command and control (C2), ammo management and positioning. When part of the striking force, plan and integrate fires as for a deliberate attack. When part of the defending force, plan and integrate fires as for an area defense. In either case, pay particular attention to the location of the converging forces and the need for an RFL.

Example EFSTs in the Defense.

Task: Delay the ability of follow-on enemy echelons to support units in contact.

Purpose: Allow defending unit to fight enemy echelons sequentially.

Method: Close air support, scatterable mines, and/or massed artillery fires at restrictive points along the enemy avenue(s) of approach. Priority of fires to COLTs until effects achieved.

Effects: Northern infantry company delayed at least 30 minutes in reaching phase line (PL) Gray. CAS destroys 4 of 4 tanks. FA destroys 2 of 5 BMPs.

Task: Disrupt ability of stationary enemy reconnaissance elements to identify and report friendly unit defensive positions.

Purpose: To preserve the security of defensive positions and maximize the effectiveness of the engagement areas.

Method: Precision munitions, artillery/mortar illumination and suppression priority targets. Each TF allocated 1 Copperhead (CPHD) target; priority for illumination to TF 2-64; each TF allocated one artillery target (battery 2 rds) for immediately responsive suppressive fires

Effects: 5 of 6 regimental reconnaissance (recon) vehicles destroyed west of PL Gray.

Task: Disrupt ability of enemy infantry to penetrate friendly defensive positions.

Purpose: Allow infantry unit to disengage from enemy forces, maneuver and reposition within the defense.

Method: Execute a linear priority target with sustained artillery or mortars fires until purpose is achieved or ammunition is depleted. Each TF allocated 1 battery FPF - direct link from FSO to battery commander authorized.

Effects: FPF is adjusted for each firing unit. Fires commence within 30 seconds of command to fire and continue until cease loading is ordered.

Delay

3-37. Attack enemy forces far forward. Suppress enemy forces and degrade their ability to maneuver. Use CAS to help disengage and slow/attrit advancing enemy forces. Use your fires as an *overwatch* element if executing a bounding overwatch type maneuver scheme. Fires can cover obstacles, gaps and flanks, provide massed fires to delay the advancing enemy, and integrate non-lethal fires, including screening fires, into the scheme. Consider the use of fires to assist in disengaging. Allocate FPFs as necessary.

Withdrawal

3-38. Have the FSO and chemical officer plan to mask the movement of friendly forces with smoke during both day and night operations. Leave the maximum number of firing units forward. Establish disengagement criteria for them and ensure this plan is rehearsed. Other considerations are similar to those for a delay.

STABILITY OPERATIONS

3-39. Non-lethal fires may be the primary means of attack in many stability operations.

Ensure the staff integrates the IO coordinator (if attached), PSYOP representative, civil affairs representative, IEW staff officer, public affairs officer, representatives from government agencies, non-governmental and possibly local civilian leadership into the concept of the operation and targeting process. What your staff does is not necessarily different in stability operations; the desired effects and assets used may be significantly different than for the offense and defense.

3-40. Use offensive lethal fires strictly in accordance with the ROE. Use defensive fires to protect the force; ROE will still apply. Plan fires for base camp defense (if base camps are used). Ensure radar zones become an integral part of the force protection plan.

3-41. As you consider the use of Firefinder radars to enhance force protection, remember that *all* acquisitions will already be a priority for action - use CFZs judiciously. Ensure censor zones are placed over friendly indirect positions - hold the FSO or targeting officer responsible for moving, confirming or canceling radar zones.

3-42. Consider dissemination of the fire support plan down through battalion, company and platoon to the leaders in charge of checkpoints, patrols and logistics convoys. Use aviation assets, if available to assist in executing the R&S plan.

3-43. Clearance of fires may include coordination with designated civilian organizations. Plan and rehearse clearance of fires drills. Establish liaison with allied military organizations to facilitate calls for fire and clearance of fires.

3-44. Consider using fires into uninhabited/unoccupied areas (possible free fire area) to demonstrate our deterrent capability (ROE dependent). The minimization of collateral damage will become a major constraint. Refer to the ROE frequently as FSCMs are established.

3-45. To demonstrate power projection, consider moving field artillery and mortar units within your zone, emplacing them, and pointing the tubes at positions that are selected to send a message to civilians and soldiers of both (all) sides.

SUPPORT OPERATIONS

3-46. Your fire support structure can support these actions by providing effective C2, observation posts, convoy operations, local security, sustainment operations and liaison capabilities. What your staff does (in terms of planning and preparing) is not necessarily different in support operations; the desired effects and assets used may be significantly different than for the offense and defense.

3-47. Non lethal fires will be the primary means of *attack* in support operations. Ensure the staff integrates the IO coordinator (if attached), PSYOP and public and civil affairs representatives, IEW staff officer, representatives from non-governmental organizations and possibly local civilian leadership into the concept of the operation and targeting process.

MOUT

3-48. The scheme of maneuver may include movement to contact or air assault (or a combination), breaching operations, a hasty or deliberate attack to seize objectives in a city or town, and providing fires for a follow-on mission - ensure the FSCOORD and FSO know to plan fires for the entire operation, not just the urban terrain phase.

3-49. The approval process based on the political sensitivity of engaging MOUT targets in certain situations can reside at command levels much higher than the requesting commander. This process, along with detailed information about the target and your intent must be completely understood by the targeting team.

TTP TIP

Target engagement in Somalia required National Command Authority (NCA) approval. Four essential elements of information had to be submitted to receive approval: military significance of the target, reliability of targeting information, extent of possible collateral damage, and, engagement weapon options. Additionally, extensive time and effort were spent researching and compiling required information concerning the characteristics and effects of munitions available in theater. IPB and target analysis were time consuming and tedious tasks, but they were necessities for the approval process from the tactical commander through the unified commander to the NCA.

3-50. Ensure the FSCOORD, FSO and battle staff have considered the following:

- What are the indirect fire ROE? What is on the restricted target list?
- Dissemination of maneuver scheme and fire support products down to the lowest level.
- Specifying who positions the COLTs/Strikers.
- What radar zones and cueing agents are required in the objective city?
- Where are the underground fuel and industrial storage tanks, gas distribution lines, gas storage tanks, and gas lines above ground?
- How has the enemy reinforced buildings?
- How will fire support and other personnel requesting fires determine 8-digit grid coordinates to targets in built-up areas?
- What is the general construction or composition of buildings, road surfaces, and barrier obstacles that require breaching? Which buildings have basements? (Collateral damage issues.)
- Which buildings/structures require large-caliber weapon/howitzer direct fire before assaulting?
- Where does tall building masking prevent indirect fire from engaging targets?
- Where are areas between tall buildings that prevent aircraft from engaging targets?
- Which sites provide the best observation posts (both friendly and enemy)? Which can be used for laser designators? Will an OH-58D be available for laser designation?
- Where to best position mortars, towed, and self-propelled (SP) artillery (both within and outside the city)? Which positions permit 6400-mil firing?
- Identify enemy mortar capability and radar zone requirements and limitations.

- Which areas of the city are most likely to be affected by the incendiary effects of detonating artillery and mortar rounds?
- Are targets outside the city to help block advancing enemy elements necessary, planned and triggers determined?
- Consider the use of smoke to obscure friendly operations from enemy observation.

3-51. ROE and restrictions on collateral damage may dictate a reliance on precision munitions. If so, ammunition resupply should become one of your priorities. Give explicit guidance on the use of, or restriction on, illumination.

TTP TIP

Bosnia/Croatia. Any building floors above the 5th floor were dealt with very effectively by artillery in both the indirect and direct fire modes. Open areas were planned targets. Adjusting fire became problematic if the observer location was not carefully chosen.

Grozny. Indirect fire was used on the approach to the city and for capturing the outskirts. The majority of self-propelled artillery was attached to the maneuver elements because artillery could elevate where tanks and BMPs could not. Direct fire was more effective in minimizing rubbling than indirect fire.

BREACHING OPERATIONS

3-52. The FSCOORD and FSO will focus on executing SOSR-related EFSTs - your guidance, especially as it relates to suppressing and obscuring (when and where, for how long) is critical. Fires support may have to execute other EFSTs while suppression and obscuration are ongoing (on-call and targets of opportunity) - how will you prioritize EFSTs throughout the breaching operation? The FSCOORD should consider requirements for force protection at the breach site. Ensure the FSO checks the dimensions of CFZ(s) established - do they account for fairly static elements waiting to go through the breach and reorganizing beyond the breach?

3-53. Have the FSCOORD/FSO consider the following:

- Use scouts or other observers to set conditions at the breach site prior to arrival of the main body. Correctly identifying where to penetrate, suppress and obscure, and communicating that information quickly, is imperative.
- Plan target handoff with observers or scouts.
- Predict likely enemy locations and plan on-call fires accordingly.
- Position observers with redundancy.
- Plan for the shifting of priority of fires to the support force, then to the assault force. What are the triggers?

- Plan and fire smoke to cover movement of the support force.
- Using obscurants for deception in order to protect the breach site.

PASSAGE OF LINES

3-54. Because of the greater range of field artillery systems, the transfer of fire support coordination responsibility may occur prior to the maneuver units' battle handover - ensure the FSCOORD has coordinated this event closely.

3-55. Information should be exchanged between the stationary and passing force's FSEs, including:

- Specific SOP information.
- Target lists and fire plans.
- Status of fire support assets.
- Attack guidance, target selection standards and engagement criteria.
- EFSTs and HPTs.
- FSCMs and maneuver control measures.
- Recognition signals.
- Information on obstacles.
- Positions for fire support assets.
- Meteorological and survey information.
- Automated database and electronic messaging information.
- · Signal operating instructions (SOI).
- ROE and security measures in effect.
- Intelligence situation.

3-56. Ensure the FSCOORD considers the following for a **Forward Passage of Lines:**

- Use of smoke to obscure enemy observers or screen friendly movement.
- The stationary force supports the close battle while the passing force's artillery moves through.
- The FSE of the passing force sends a liaison to the FSE of the stationary force.
- The CFL is continually updated. FSOs must know the lead element's position continuously.
- Fire support assets should be positioned near the passage point without interfering with the passage of lines. Give priority of positioning to the passing force.
- Ensure passing force plans fires to support operations after the passage of lines.

3-57. Ensure the FSCOORD considers the following for a **Rearward Passage of Lines**.

- Use of smoke to conceal movement through passage points.
- Planned fires to support disengagement of forces and the deception plan (if part of the concept of operation).
- Ensure counterfire actions are planned and controlled by the stationary force.
- Give priority of positioning to the stationary force.

- The FSE of the stationary force sends a liaison to the FSE of the passing force.

AIRBORNE OPERATIONS

3-58. Conduct of fire support coordination distinguishes the initial assault phase from subsequent phases. During the assault phase, C2 is conducted from an airborne platform. The FSCOORD/FSO should review SEAD requirements in support of the air movement plan. Fire support planning and coordination functions are transferred to the ground force when the assaulting force commander and his FSO are on the ground and operational. FSE personnel should be cross-loaded in the landing plan so that loss of an aircraft does not completely disrupt fire support provided to the assaulting force.

3-59. At first, the assaulting force FSO is more concerned with close-in targets, while the airborne FSE focuses on deeper targets. Initial targeting intelligence is likely to come from national assets. Information links to the FSE must be thoroughly reviewed and understood by the targeting team. Fire planning for the ground tactical plan should consider EFSTs that support of the concept of operation and those that support defending the airhead.

3-60. Have the FSCOORD and FSO consider the following when planning fire support for an airborne operation:

- Positioning of artillery and mortars inside the airhead line to provide continuous 6400-mil fires without adversely impacting on airfield operations.
- Centralized control of fires.
- Minimum indirect fire ranges.
- A2C2.
- Tactical cross-loads.
- Assault command post (ACP) operations.
- Use of permissive FSCM to facilitate tactical air attacks.
- RFAs around the airfield to reduce cratering and other collateral damage.
- Use of long-range surveillance detachment (LRSD)/ long-range surveillance unit (LRSU) for target acquisition.

AIR ASSAULT OPERATIONS

3-61. Not only should fire support be synchronized with the ground tactical plan, landing plan and air movement plan, but ammunition resupply procedures must be carefully integrated into the operation due to limited haul capacity.

3-62. Have the FSCOORD and FSO consider the following when planning fire support for an air assault operation:

- Will the landing zone be prepared with pre-planned fires? Is lethal SEAD required?
- Will false landing zones be utilized? If so, are false preparations desired?

- Where are the flight routes in relation to planned targets and delivery assets? Determine flight times, checkpoints, and code words.
- How are air defense systems being targeted? How will they be destroyed or suppressed? For how long (if suppression is called for)?
- What are the abort criteria?
- What A2C2 measures will be required?
- Will additional detect/assess or deliver assets be required from higher headquarters?
- Input for air mission briefing.
- Command and control considerations to include an effective plan to request and clear fires given various cross-loads of personnel and communications equipment.

3-63. Fire planning procedures, the targeting process, and targeting products are conducted/developed as for any operation with special consideration of the above.

Chapter 4

FIRE SUPPORT TECHNIQUES AND PROCEDURES

"I emphasized meticulous planning not simply because I thought it was the most effective approach, which it is, but because by taking that approach you enforce on your subordinates the same necessity. They have to learn every detail of the topography, every position, every soldier they will be facing. And once they do that, they will be able to decide rationally - not intuitively - on the steps they will have to take. They will make their decisions on the basis of knowledge. Experience has taught me that if you lay your plans in detail before you are under the stress of fighting, the chances are much greater that you will be able to implement at least the outline of the plans despite the contingencies of battle."

General Ariel Sharon,
Warrior, 1989

4-1. Synchronizing fires and maneuver is difficult enough even under the most favorable conditions. Its attainment becomes decidedly less likely if not properly planned and prepared for. This chapter presents you with procedures and techniques for better integrating fires with your scheme of maneuver during the MDMP. It also discusses the integration of targeting into both the MDMP and unit battle rhythm, and subsequently, gives you procedures for preparing for combat. The chapter concludes with procedures for the execution of fires and fire support-related actions during mission operations.

PLANNING

Military Decision Making Process

4-2. The MDMP per FM 5-0 (101-5), *Staff Organization and Operations,* presents a process to properly integrate all BOS into a military operation. No changes are required of that process to achieve synchronization between fires and maneuver. What is required, though, is close attention to detail, especially by the staff, and a working knowledge of the inputs, actions and outputs presented under each of the MDMP steps below.

Mission Analysis

4-3. The FSE conducts the fire support portion of mission analysis as part of the battle staff. The following chart depicts inputs coming in to the fire support element, what actions they take, what they produce and your impact, as depicted in the **YOUR INPUT** column, on this step:

INPUTS TO FSE	ACTIONS	OUTPUTS	YOUR INPUT	NEXT ACTION
-Higher HQ OPORD -Facts from higher, lower, adjacent FSEs -IPB Products – see next page -Facts from FS assets	-Understand higher OPORD -Organize and analyze facts -Identify specified and implied tasks -Translate status of FS assets into capabilities -Analyze effects of IPB on FS. -Develop Draft EFSTs	-FS portion of mission analysis brief -Recommend EFSTs -Draft R&S plan	-Demand detail in the mission analysis briefing -Approve or modify draft EFSTs -Give your intent -Give planning guidance, to include FS guidance, to the battle staff	-Modify outputs based on Cdr's input -Issue warning order (WARNO) -Begin COA development -Develop fire support plan to support R&S plan

TTP TIP

The top-down fire planning process began with the issuance of the warning order immediately following mission analysis. The FSO should ensure that the approved draft EFSTs are part of the WARNO. By doing this the FSO allows suboardinate commanders and FSOs to begin framing their fire support plan not only within their own concepts of operation, but in concert with the higher headquarters' fire support plan. Later in the planning and preparation process, suboardinate FSOs offer refinement by requesting EFSTs not covered in the higher headquarters' plan

IPB

4-4. This critical part of mission analysis involves input from the entire staff, including the FSO. While the S2 is piecing together the enemy situation, he requires assistance from each BOS. The FSO and DS Battalion S2 should be refining the situation template for enemy fire support systems; the ALO, ADA officer and Aviation LNO (if present) should be refining the situation template (SITTEMP) for enemy air defense systems; and so forth. This will help ensure the best basis for the remainder of the MDMP and targeting process is available.

4-5. Situation templates are the start points for the targeting effort. Poor templates used later in the wargaming process, or during targeting meetings, will result in ineffective targeting. There is no limit (other than time) on the number of SITTEMPs that can be developed. Consider developing several templates for each enemy COA (under current procedures normally just one is developed). In this manner, you will be able to base your concept of the operation and targeting decisions on how the enemy will look **when** you want to attack them.

4-6. IPB products include a HVT list (those assets that the enemy commander requires to successfully complete his mission); enemy COAs [description and graphical depiction (situation template)]; and event templates (SITTEMPs overlayed to determine NAIs - though this product will continue to be revised).

- Selected HVTs become high-payoff targets and EFSTs through wargaming and subsequent targeting meetings.
- Enemy COAs form the basis for friendly COA development as initial targeting decisions are recommended (what to attack with whom).
- Event templates form the basis for the initial R&S plan and are further developed during COA analysis.

Commander's Intent

Commanders Intent is described as a *"...clear, concise statement of what the force must do to succeed with respect to the enemy and the terrain and the desired end state. It provides the link between the mission and the concept of operations by stating the key tasks that, along with the mission, are the basis for subordinates to exercise initiative when unanticipated opportunities arise or when the original concept of operations no long r applies..."*

> *FM 101-5, Staff Organization and Operations, 31 May 1997*

4-8. Long, vague intent statements detract from synchronization by *fogging-up* how you see maneuver and fires working together. If it's not clear to you, it's probably not clear to your S3, FSCOORD, or FSO, either. There is no commander's intent for fires. There is but one intent statement per commander, nested in the higher headquarters' concept of operations, and providing the foundation for a comprehensive concept of operations that will be the basis for your subordinate commander's intent statement. Though you do not give a separate intent for fires, you provide guidance to the FSCOORD as discussed below.

Commander's Guidance for Fire Support

4-9. Guidance to the FSCOORD does not have to be any different than the guidance you give to your subordinate maneuver commanders: give him doctrinally stated **tasks and purposes**. A task for fire support describes a targeting effect against a specific enemy formation's function or capability. The purpose describes how this effect contributes to accomplishing the mission within your intent. Your initial planning guidance for fire support will become the basis for the concept of fires and the fires paragraph. Synchronization in your plan will depend largely on your ability to issue planning guidance to BOS representatives that cause them to develop integrated COAs.

4-10. Consider the following when deciding what to issue for fire support guidance:

- Preferred FS system for the engagement of HPTs. Though the HPTL has not been developed/approved yet, based on the S2's mission analysis briefing you may have an idea of what asset to use (lethal fires, non-lethal fires) and desired effects against potential HPTs.
- Guidance for fires. Consider stating the **task** as an effect on the enemy (per FM 3-100.40, FM 6-20-10, FM 3-09 and FM 3-13) formation (specific element or sub-element of the enemy) that provides the enemy a function (a capability of the formation that is needed for it to achieve its primary task and purpose). State the **purpose** in terms of how the targeting effect will benefit a friendly maneuver formation. Example: Disrupt the ability of SA-7s and 14s to engage lift helicopters from pickup zone (PZ) Blue to landing zone (LZ) X-Ray **(task)** to allow the air assault task force to arrive at the LZ with at least 90% of its forces intact **(purpose).**

TTP TIP

Under severe planning time constraints, another procedure to consider is to relate a specific task and purpose for each fire support asset (field artillery, mortars, close air support, naval gunfire, electronic attack, offensive IO and so forth) to each phase of the operation. This also serves, then, as guidance for subordinate maneuver commanders and their staffs/FSEs to give them an idea of what fire support assets will be doing (for them) throughout the operation.

- Observer plan. Employment of COLTs or Strikers.
- Special Munitions - illumination use, smoke/white phosphorus (WP), ground and air launched precision guided munitions, scatterable mines.
- Counterfire or counterbattery responsibilities you want planned by the FSCOORD. (Must be synched with higher HQ or the counterfire HQ). Guidance on the establishment of (CFZ and call-for-fire zones (CFFZ). Guidance for the security of Firefinder radars (which forces at what time or event?).
- Suppression or destruction of enemy air defense guidance.
- Fire support coordinating measures.
- Protected target list. ROE guidance.
- Guidance for FPFs, minimum safe distances and risk estimate distances.
- Engagement criteria. Guidance on size and type of units you want fires to engage at select points in the operation. (for example: counter-reconnaissance - FA can be used against single, stationary lightly-armored vehicles; main battle area (MBA) - Do not plan on using FA against single vehicles unless a commander requests it.)

COA Development

4-11. As the battle staff begins the steps of COA development, the FSO must conceptualize how to integrate fires into the developing concept of operations. The start points for where and how the FSO recommends the allocation of fire support assets to each COA are the draft EFSTs and commander's guidance for fire support. The fire support endstate for this step of the MDMP is the development of draft fire support plan(s). The targeting process (decide, detect, deliver, assess) begins during this step of the MDMP (more on targeting in a subsequent section).

4-12. COA development should consider the use of all fire support systems, not just field artillery. All members of the targeting team should contribute during COA. Major movement and repositioning of fire support assets during the operation must be considered because they impact the tempo of the operation.

4-13. The following chart depicts fire support inputs, actions, and outputs for COA development and your role in this step:

INPUTS TO FSE	ACTIONS	OUTPUTS	YOUR INPUT	NEXT ACTION
-**FS** portion of mission analysis brief -**Approved EFSTs** -**Commander's** guidance for fire support	-**Determine** where to find and attack EFST formations -**Identify** HPTs in those formations -**Quantify** effects for EFSTs -**Plan** methods for EFSTs -**Allocate** assets to acquire -**Allocate** assets to attack -**Integrate** triggers with maneuver COA -**Use** battle calculus -**Assist** S2 in R&S plan development	For each COA develop a draft fire support plan that includes: -Concept of fires -Draft FSEM -Draft target list -Draft TSM or modified TSM	**Approve or modify the draft EFSTs, as part of approving COAs, that will be analyzed in the next step.**	-**Modify** outputs based on Cdr's input -**Issue** WARNO -**Prepare** for and conduct COA analysis

EFSTs - Essential Fire Support Tasks
HPT - High-Payoff Targets
COA - Course of Action
R&S - Reconnaissance and Surveillance
FSEM - Fire Support Execution Matrix
TSM- Target Synchronization Matrix
Note: Examples of these and other planning products are in Appendix B.

Positioning Fire Support Assets and Observation Planning

4-14. General positioning requirements should be worked out in COA development - these will be refined during the wargame. Have the FSO obtain the position area overlay and/or Paladin axis developed by the DS battalion during its artillery IPB process to assist in coordinating position areas.

4-15. Terrain management considerations should include the following: Locations of delivery units, radars, TOCs, and trains; movement routes and times (will be worked out in detail in the wargame); supply routes; axis for Paladin unit moves (if this procedure is followed).

4-16. Observation planning at brigade begins during this step and addresses those portions of the decide step of targeting that deal with deciding who will observe the target and initiate fires (BRT, Striker, COLT, radar, subordinate units or some other agency) and who will perform BDA (effects). Details of these decisions are worked out in the wargame. General positioning considerations to support the initial observation plan should be considered in COA development

---

TTP TIP

As the number of EFSTs, and consequent HPTs, grows during the COA development step and you quickly exhaust the number of brigade-level collection assets to detect and assess those HPTs, consider task-organizing subordinate fire support teams under brigade control, at least for those phases prior to their expected use by battalions and companies. A battalion in reserve, or in a follow (or follow and support) mission may be best suited. The alternative is to task subordinate battalions to execute brigade EFSTs, and then be dependent on their observation plan for the execution of certain essential brigade tasks. The most effective way to synchronize the observation plan is to assign target execution responsibilities to maneuver commanders in paragraph 3.b, tasks to maneuver units, of the OPORD/fragmentary order (FRAGO) and ensure that their elements are properly task organized with appropriate observation capabilities.

COA Analysis and COA Comparison

4-17. The wargame gives the staff the tools to work out virtually all details of the concept of operation. It is also during the wargame that the remainder of the targeting decisions are finalized (pending your approval). As the staff conducts an action-reaction/counteraction drill to cause and respond to enemy acts, the targeting team addresses those actions, in accordance with the scheme of maneuver and concept of fires, that must be executed.

4-18. You can check the thoroughness of the wargame by ensuring the following questions can be answered *for each EFST:*

- What is the task and purpose?
- What effects do we want to achieve?
- Where will we first detect the target?
- Who will detect it?
- When do we expect to detect it?

- When is the latest we can detect it and still attack it to achieve the purpose?
- From where will we detect it?
- How will the detect asset get to its observation location (mode and route)? How long does it take to move there? When must it leave? Does it require security and log support? From whom, when, and where?
- Is the asset detecting the target the same as the one tracking it and initiating fires on it? If so, what is the trigger to attack? If not, who is detecting, who is tracking, who is initiating fires, and how is the information passed among them?
- Is there a backup designated to detect, track and initiate fires? If so, ask the above questions about the backup. If not, why not? What asset/unit will attack the target?
- From where will they attack it? Do they have to move to attack the target? On what route, and for how long? When would they have to initiate movement?
- When will they attack the target? When is the latest they can attack the target and still achieve the purpose?
- Is there another asset designated to attack the target (backup or secondary)? If so, then when, what is the latest time for their attack? If there is no back up, why not?
- Does the attack of the target necessitate any prerequisite actions for the maneuver staff? What are the details of the prerequisite actions?
- Who will assess effects? From where? When?
- How will BDA get reported and to whom? Who will make a re-attack decision? When is the latest desired effects can be achieved through re-attack and still fulfill the purpose of attacking the target?
- How will the results of attacking this target get disseminated to the maneuver unit whose scheme of maneuver is affected by the capabilities this target possesses? (Both command and fire support channels?)

4-19. Depicted in the chart below are the inputs, actions, and outputs for the FSE during COA analysis. Your input for this step is, as part of approving the wargame, modifying and/or approving the final drafts of the fire support plans - one per COA wargamed.

INPUTS TO FSE	ACTIONS	OUTPUTS	YOUR INPUT	NEXT ACTION
For each COA to be wargamed: **-Concept of fires** **-Draft FSEM** **-Draft target list** **-Draft TSM or modified TSM** **-R&S Plan** **-Requested EFSTs from subordinates**	**-Targeting** decisions: finalize HPTL **-Wargame** fire support plan(s) against enemy COAs **-Modify/refine** inputs as required **-Refine** and test fire support plan	Final drafts of: **-Fires** paragraph **-Fire support** annex to include: **-FSEM** **-Target** List **-Target** overlay **-TSM** or modified TSM	**Approve wargame if not a participant**	**-Modify** outputs based on Cdr's input **-Prepare** COA decision briefing

4-20. By this time in the planning process, subordinate units should have developed at least draft EFSTs in support of their concept of operation. Some of these subordinate units EFSTs are refinements to the EFSTs your headquarters sent in WARNOs. Other EFSTs are submitted for your staff's consideration because your scheme of fire support did not adequately support the subordinate unit's scheme of maneuver. The staff must integrate all EFSTs into the wargame and determine either how to execute each one, or, which EFSTs cannot be executed due to lack or resources. Subordinate commanders should be immediately notified which of their requested EFSTs are not in the higher headquarters scheme of fires (your staff should be informing you also for your approval).

COA Approval and Essential Fire Support Tasks

4-21. During this step, you are approving the fire support plan as part of the approved course of action. Inherent in your approval is the assignment of essential fire support tasks to subordinate or supporting units.

4-22. EFSTs for your plan have been under development and revision since mission analysis. By this time, they ought to be in the format in which they will appear in the OPORD. Within each phase of an operation, each E FST will be described in the sequenceof planned execution using a TASK, PURPOSE, METHOD, EFFECTS format.

4-23. The FSE will use the inputs and actions depicted below to produce outputs for your consideration. *Your approval of the course of action indicates you are satisfied with the degree of synchronization between maneuver and fires that the plan contains.*

INPUTS TO FSE	ACTIONS	OUTPUTS	YOUR INPUT	NEXT ACTION
-Fires paragraph -Fire support annex to include: -FSEM -Target List -Target overlay -TSM or modified TSM	-Approval briefing -Fire support plan briefed as part of each COA -FSCOORD may present analysis as part of the staff	-Commander modifies or approves COA -Issue WARNO -Finalize fire support products -Issue OPORD as part of the staff -Conduct fire support backbriefs	-Demand detail in the COA approval briefing Approve/ modify fire support plan as part of the approved COA	-Manage refinement -Prepare OPORD and briefing products -Conduct rehearsals

Orders Briefing

4-24. The primary audience for the fire support portion of this briefing is the commanders or supervisors of those units/individuals responsible for executing EFSTs. The following should be considered during the fire support portion of the OPORD briefing:

- Scheme of fires (includes logical sequence of EFSTs).

- Clearance of fires procedures (if different than SOP).
- FSCMs and restrictions.
- Cutoff times for target refinement and battalion requests for brigade planned fires.
- Rehearsal instructions.
- *Always include in your OPORD confirmation brief a review of EFST responsibilities (who has primary and backup trigger/observation responsibility for TAI or targets; who is firing what munition from where, when; who assess effects, when, how, and from where).*

The Targeting Process and the MDMP

4-25. The targeting process is not a distinct series of actions that occur exclusive of the MDMP. Instead, the targeting process (D3A) begins as

DECIDE *decisions* are made while the staff is conducting the MDMP. Since the battle staff is the targeting team, if the staff conducts the MDMP properly, there is no need during the MDMP to conduct a separate targeting meeting - the results of what the targeting meeting would give you are already being developed as the plan is being built. The chart on the next page depicts how the targeting process fits within the MDMP and the unit's battle rhythm. Targeting during mission execution is covered in more detail later in this chapter.

MDMP Step	Receipt of Mission	Mission Analysis	COA Development	COA Analysis	COA Approval & Orders	Rehearsals	Execution & Assesment
Targeting Process Function	Assemble Target Team[1]	Initial DECIDE[2] Initial DETECT (R&S Plan)	Draft DECIDE[3]	Refine DECIDE[4]	DECIDE Function Continues[5]	Possible Targeting Meeting[6]	DETECT DELIVER ASSESS[7] Targeting Meeting[8]
Targeting Products[11]		HVTs Draft EFSTs	Draft FSEM Draft HPTL Draft TSM Draft R&S Plan	FSEM HPTL TSM R&S Plan		Refined: FSEM HPTL TSM R&S Plan	Refined: FSEM HPTL TSM R&S Plan
Unit Battle Rhythm	Plan	Plan Execute R&S Plan	Plan	Plan	Plan	Prepare & Plan[9]	Execute & plan[10]

Notes:

1. When separate targeting meetings are convened, the targeting team = battle staff (include non-lethal reps; reference Chapter 2)

2. The initial DECIDE factors developed here are based on enemy COA development, draft EFSTs, other specified and essential tasks, and status of detect and deliver assets.

3. Draft DECIDE factors should address what, how, when, and where to detect an EFST formation; what, how, when, and where to attack that EFST formation; and what, how, when, and where to assess the attack on that EFST formation. Draft HPTs are developed to clarify the EFST.

4. Refined DECIDE factors should address the what, how, when, and where to detect, attack and assess each HPT associated with an EFST.

5. The decisions made up to the point of COA approval and the production of an OPORD form the basis for change for targeting products. Rehearsals, friendly and enemy situation updates, subsequent targeting meetings, and so forth. all can modify previous decisions.

6. If the time between OPORD dissemination and rehearsals allows for the friendly, and especially the enemy, situation to change, or as part of your unit's daily battle rhythm (see note 9), revisit previously made targeting decisions during a targeting meeting.

7. During execution, the DETECT, DELIVER, and ASSESS functions of targeting are conducted in accordance with the concept of operation (as modified by the existing situation) and the commander's intent in a synchronized manner with the scheme of maneuver.

8. Normally, daily and/or event-driven targeting meetings are conducted during execution.

9. Refinements to the current plan continue until the mission is accomplished.

10. During execution, planning continues on branches and sequels to the base plan (tied in with note 8); or, a new mission is received and the MDMP (with its own embedded targeting process) initiated.

11. Brigade is normally the lowest level at which all or most of these products are tangibly produced.

PREPARATION

4-26. Once a synchronized plan has been developed, the unit focuses on the preparation phase of operations. Two key events occur here that have the capability of adding to the level of synchronization between maneuver and fires for the upcoming mission: the combined arms rehearsal and the process of target refinement.

Combined Arms Rehearsals

4-27. The maneuver unit headquarters normally conducts the combined arms rehearsal after subordinate units have issued their OPORD/FASP. This rehearsal ensures that the subordinate units' plans are synchronized with those of the other units in the organization and that those plans will achieve the intent of the higher commander. *A fire support rehearsal should be conducted **prior to** the combined arms rehearsal and if possible should include the maneuver S2 and S3 and other members of the targeting team as appropriate.*

4-28. Key fire support points that should be addressed during the combined arms rehearsal include:

- Responsibilities and actions for the execution of EFSTs, with triggers.
- Positioning and movement plans for fire support assets, with triggers.
- Verification of the R&S plan to support targeting and the target acquisition plan to support counterbattery fire, to include radar zone management, with triggers.
- Current and planned fire support coordinating measures, with triggers and procedures for changing/moving.
- Clearance of fires procedures.
- CAS and JAAT actions, with A2C2 measures and ACA, SEAD and other enablers.

TTP TIP

Have the individual(s) responsible for executing the method of EFSTs participate in the rehearsal. It detracts from synchronization if, for example, the S2 depicts an enemy action that triggers an attack by fires and the FSO explains that COLT 1 has observed the action, will initiate planned artillery fires, and will assess whether X effects were achieved. The FSO is not executing the task, therefore he should not be practicing it at the rehearsal.

The Fire Planning Process

4-29. Fire planning is a continuous process of planning and coordinating fire support requirements. It is usually top-down driven or initiated (exception being a quick fire plan). Central to the process is the development and execution of EFSTs. Conceptually, a fire plan is the logical sequence of executing EFSTs to support a concept of operation. A fire plan at any level is normally the sum of fire support tasks you receive from higher (these are almost always essential to you), EFSTs you develop, and fire support tasks requested by your subordinates.

4-30. A battalion (task force) must clearly understand not only the brigade concept of fires and how it is synchronized to support brigade maneuver but also the battalion's role in the brigade scheme of fires so that the battalion can execute its portion. The battalion must also develop its own concept of fires involving EFSTs assigned from brigade and targets to support the battalion close/direct fire fight. The battalion scheme of fires (including both brigade and battalion targets) is passed down to the companies where another level of refinement is conducted. After the companies refine and forward their fire support requests to battalion, the battalion consolidates, resolves duplications and forwards the battalion concept of fires and target refinements to brigade.

4-31. The following chart depicts brigade and battalion roles in this process.

Brigade Role in Fire Support Planning	Battalion Role in Fire Support Planning
-Synchronize the brigade concept of fires with brigade maneuver -Develop brigade scheme of fires and assign EFSTs to subordinates -Provide fire support for battalion close/direct fire fight -Integrate refinements from subordinates -Integrate movement of fire support assets into the scheme of maneuver	-Understand the integration of brigade maneuver and fires -Understand battalion role in the brigade scheme of fires/maneuver -Execute assigned EFSTs -Develop battalion concept and scheme of fires -Integrate and refine brigade EFSTs for close/direct fire fight -Plan for the synchronization of battalion mortars with the scheme of fires and their movement with the scheme of maneuver -Manage refinement from companies -Forward battalion concept of fires and target refinements to brigade

4-32. Initial targeting decisions are based on templates that must be refined through execution of the R&S plan and analysis of reported intelligence data. As more accurate information on the enemy is obtained, target lists must be updated and disseminated. Target data refinement considerations include:

- Changing target locations, but not the purpose of the target. The purpose of the target was established during the MDMP and is linked to the EFST for which that target was developed. Changing the purpose implies a new EFST and involves commander, or at least S3, approval.
- Enforce target refinement cutoff times. Target cutoff is the latest time when a higher FSE will accept information changes on targets (location being the most prevalent) from a lower FSE. Cutoff times are established to ensure all commanders, fire supporters target acquirers and key decision-makers have the **single approved** target list/scheme of fires prior to an operation starting. This does not preclude the attack of targets of opportunity, but it does allow for proper positioning of fire support assets based on the location of planned targets assigned to those assets and allows for the most accurate location to be disseminated to the delivery assets-a critical factor when fires are initiated using a target number vice grid coordinate

EXECUTION

4-33. During a battle, the positioning of the FSCOORD and FSO is dependent on your location (normally the FSCOORD is with you) and whether you have established a tactical (TAC) CP (normally the FSO will accompany the S3 at the TAC CP). Regardless, during execution they should be able to tell you at any given time, much like a subordinate maneuver commander, the status of fire support assets and what fires are doing. The following paragraphs discuss procedures for common fire support-related activities that occur during mission execution.

Focusing Fires and the Brigade and Task Force Fights

4-34. As EFSTs are determined during the MDMP using a top-down planning, bottom-up refinement process, fires are integrated into the scheme of maneuver. If the staff has thoroughly wargamed possible enemy and friendly courses of action, the resultant fire support plan is focused. That is, it provides the effects desired by the commander when and where he wants them to help accomplish the mission. During execution, the only thing that should be allowed to desynchronize the plan is (are) enemy actions not previously considered. Since this will almost always occur, you must have a system in place to immediately make D3A decisions, disseminate them and execute them violently. Fighting the enemy (not the plan) in accordance with your guidance provides focus.

4-35. In terms of a *brigade versus battalion fight*, there is only one fire plan. The top-down plan developed and refined during the MDMP and preparation phase should incorporate EFSTs supporting brigade and battalion (and company) schemes of maneuver. As (if) fires shift from deeper to closer targets, execution responsibility tends to shift from brigade to battalion. In executing the fire plan, brigade *does not hand fires off to subordinate headquarters, it hands off the responsibility for executing certain EFSTs to subordinate headquarters*. In this manner, brigade fires remain synchronized with brigade maneuver - while still supporting subordinate maneuver units. The expected conflict between simultaneously attacking targets the battalion wants attacked by fires and targets the brigade wants attacked by fires must be planned for and wargamed in the MDMP.

Clearance of Fires

4-36. Maneuver commanders clear fires. Normally, managing this is delegated to their main command posts and executed by the battle staff under the lead of the FSE. In either analog or digital operations, **silence is not consent** - clearance of fires requires positive action. **The clearance of fires begins with receipt of the mission and is a part of every step in the MDMP.**

4-37. The first step in effective clearance of fires is the use of maneuver control measures. Any time you can procedurally depict ownership of land the better for clearing fires. If no boundaries are established, all fires short of the CFL (if established) must be cleared by the higher headquarters instead of the headquarters closest to the fires. While clearing fires is potentially more complicated in distributed, non-linear operations, serious consideration should be given for establishing areas of operation for each subordinate maneuver unit, consistent with the scheme of maneuver.

4-38. Proper use of FSCMs also facilitates the clearance of fires. Permissive measures (if positioned correctly and disseminated to all higher, adjacent, and subordinate units), such as CFLs and free fire areas (FFAs), offer the opportunity for safe responsive fires on targets of opportunity. The size of restrictive measures (no fire area (NFA), RFA) should be verified to preclude unwarranted delays for otherwise safe fires. The next section contains more information on managing FSCMs.

4-39. Pre-clearing fires is one of the most effective ways to ensure troop safety and speed up target engagement.. Units should clear fires during the planning phase. Two instances are: (1) fires into a planned call for fire zone (CFFZ) resulting from a radar acquisition from that planned CFFZ - the CFFZ must have been planned in advance and published in the radar deployment order; and (2) fires on preplanned target, with a definable trigger, against a specific enemy, and according to the scheme of fire support. Other pre-cleared fires should be stated in specific terms. For example, "AB 3001 is pre-cleared through the end of Phase I." Always ensure pre-clearance is disseminated in plans and orders and included in all rehearsals. The more pre-clearance work done in preparation the less delay experienced in execution.

4-40. When fires are requested that are not pre-cleared or allowed by a permissive fire support coordinating measure, they must be positively cleared. This procedure can, in fact, should be a battle drill in command posts.

4-41. In an analog TOC, clearing fires off the situation map is **not** recommended - it will seldom be accurate enough to guarantee the safety of friendly soldiers. Calls for clearance should originate from the requesting maneuver force (probably made by the FSO) over both the fire support net and either the command or operations and intelligence (O&I) net. The TOC responsible for clearing fires should make an Attention in the TOC announcement, read the grid of the target, and get an answer from each BOS representative that no friendlies of that BOS are in danger. **simultaneously**, the TOC initiates a radio net call, over both command and fire support nets, requesting the ground commander(s) to clear a particular grid for attack with a particular asset. (for example., **"Guidons, this is V27, clear fires for grid PU346745, 120mm mortars, over"**). Each company commander reads back the grid location and fire support asset and clears or denies the mission. The TOC then reports back over both nets that the target is clear (or denied).

4-42. In a digital TOC with situational awareness maintained through Force XXI Battle Command Brigade and Below (FBCB2) or similar technology, clearance of fires must be addressed the same as above. Unless you can guarantee that every friendly element (including vehicles and dismounts) in your zone has electronically provided their location (not just the FBCB2-equipped, organic units), a drill similar to that discussed for analog operations should be conducted.

4-43. The AFATDS can both assist and hinder in clearance of fires procedures. It assists by automatically sending a digital request for coordination (clearance) when fires are requested cross-boundary or when an FSCM is violated by a request for fires. The clearance drill must still be accomplished with the responsible TOC, then the results transmitted digitally to the originator. AFATDS can hinder rapid clearance of fires by automatically intervening on calls for fires based on improper, or inaccurate, intervention criteria and safe distance radii relating to FSCM establishment. Ensure your FSO reviews these data closely.

Managing Fire Support Coordinating Measures

4-44. The purpose of this section is to present you with tactical considerations for the placement and size of FSCMs you approve. For FSCM definitions and graphics, see FM 6-20-40, *Tactics, Techniques, and Procedures for Fire Support for Heavy Brigade Operations*.

4-45. When considering the coordinated fire line, there is no requirement to place the CFL on identifiable terrain. Use phase lines as CFLs only if the placement makes sense based on the targets you want to attack with surface fires. If the CFL is placed beyond the concentration of enemy mortars that comprise an EFST, then every Firefinder radar detection will have to be cleared before counterfire can be brought to bear (unless the mortars are in a pre-cleared CFFZ). Friendlies can operate beyond the CFL - they should be protected, though, with NFAs or RFAs and their movements strictly controlled. Cover the trigger(s) and changing of CFLs at combined arms rehearsals to synchronize subordinate commander's scheme of maneuver with targeting team efforts.

4-46. Considerations for NFAs, RFAs and RFLs must include the size of these areas. They should be just large enough to safeguard the force, element, or individual for which they are established. An NFA with a 1km radius established over a COLT position offers a *buffer zone* about five times larger than it needs to be to protect the COLT (munition dependent). With AFATDS, if that observer buffer zone is touched by the artificial criteria of the input target buffer zone (a radius around the target that approximates a particular munition's effects), the mission will be delayed for coordination. As discussed in the clearance of fires section, have the FSO closely review and validate NFA/RFA size as well as target buffer zone inputs for the various munitions. RFLs should be placed on recognizable terrain and are established by the commander common to the converging forces. Consider their use in virtually all offensive operations that entail a support by fire and a maneuver force and in distributed operations where higher headquarters scouts may be operating in your area of operations.

4-471. Formal airspace coordination areas may be recommended at your level, but the air control authority (also ACA) approves them at the air operations center (AOC). Informal ACAs are discussed in the section on CAS integration.

Counterfire and Radar Zone Management

4-48. First and foremost - **if no radar zones are established, Firefinder radars will still acquire targets** (if it is cueing) and will pass the intelligence to the artillery TOC (it can be converted to a call for fire and fired at that time). All the establishment of critical friendly zones (CFZ) and call for fire zones (CFFZ) does is change the format of the Firefinder report to a call for fire and place a higher priority on it. This method allows the initial fire support automation system (IFSAS) and AFATDS to handle it as soon as its received. Still, the proper establishment of radar zones can expedite the reactive counterfire process. See Appendix E for more information on radar zones.

4-49. Consider these factors when establishing zones:

- In the offense, are breach sites and areas directly leading in and out covered by CFZ?
- Can assembly areas, assault and attack positions get CFZ coverage?
- Will a CFZ be placed on the objective(s) during consolidation?
- Are support by fire positions covered with CFZ?

A2C2 and CAS Integration Considerations

4-52. A2C2 procedures and measures are covered in detail in FM 100-13-1 and in general in FM 6-20-40. If you have air assets task organized [including unmanned aerial vehicle (UAV)], your A2C2 element will not only have to deconflict air control measures with division, but also with your scheme of fires to provide uninterrupted air and fire support. (Another opportunity to *overlay the overlays*.)

4-53. Four standard procedures exist to integrate UAV, CAS, and artillery fires with a minimum of disruption: lateral, altitude, time, and, altitude and lateral separation. These are informal airspace coordination measures. If properly planned and coordinated, CAS should not cause indirect fire support to stop, and vice versa.

- Lateral Separation. Used to attack two targets that are close together, one with CAS and the other with artillery. The forward air controller obtains gun-target line information, and passes this to the aircraft to prevent it from crossing the line. This procedure can also be expanded to separate portions of engagement areas for specific weapons.

- Altitude Separation. Used to attack the same target. The maximum and minimum ordinates are passed to the forward air controller so that aircraft stay above/stay below the trajectory of the artillery rounds.
- Time Separation. Used to attack either the same target with different means or several targets in the same engagement area. Indirect fires are controlled by an *At My Command* method of control; CAS is controlled by instructions in the 9-line brief. Indirect fires are dependent on CAS and fired when the airspace is clear until the next sortie arrives.
- Altitude and Lateral Separation. Used to attack several targets within a relatively small area. Also used to provide SEAD fires when the CAS target is between the artillery gun positions and enemy ADA positions. Combines the techniques discussed under the separate headings above.

The Targeting Process During Mission Execution

4-54. During the execution phase of operations, the battle staff (targeting team) is continually assessing the current situation, tracking decision points, possibly preparing some type of update briefing for the commander, and looking towards the future (whether that is 6 to 36 or more hours depends on the level of command and situation). The targeting process allows you to extend the MDMP throughout your operation by giving you a forum to reconsider *who kills who* decisions and modify or initiate actions to implement those decisions. The process normally occurs within the setting of (informal) targeting meetings. At battalion level, an abbreviated form of a targeting meeting is generally used.

Targeting Meetings

4-55. The targeting meeting is an important event in the unit's battle rhythm. It focuses and synchronizes the unit's combat power and resources toward finding, tracking, attacking, and assessing HPT. The meeting:

- Verifies and updates the HPTL.
- Verifies, updates and re-tasks available collection assets for each HPT.
- Allocates delivery systems to engage each target.
- Confirms the assets tasked to verify the effects on target after it has been attacked.
- Provides a forum for target attack nominations by joint systems.
- Synchronizes lethal and non-lethal actions (to include IO).

4-56. To be effective, if a separate targeting meeting is held, the following personnel should attend the meeting:

- Brigade commander (when available).
- Brigade XO (runs the meeting).
- FSCOORD.
- Brigade S3 (runs the meeting in the XO's absence).
- Brigade S2.

- ALO.
- IO coordinator (if present).
- Brigade S4.
- Brigade Engineer (Assistant Brigade Engineer/Engineer LNO in his absence).
- Brigade ADA Officer (assistant brigade ADAO/ADA LNO in his absence).
- Aviation LNO.
- Brigade S3 Air.
- MI company commander.
- BRT commander and Striker platoon leader.
- Chemical Officer.
- Tactical PSYOP detachment commander.
- Civil Affairs team leader.
- FSO.
- Targeting Officer.
- DS FA battalion S2 (if available).
- SJA .

TTP TIP

At battalion level an ad-hoc targeting group consisting of the Commander, S2, S3, and FSO is often used to make targeting decisions in an informal targeting meeting.

4-57. The timing of the targeting meeting is critical. It must be effectively integrated into the unit's battle rhythm and nested in the higher headquarters' targeting cycle to ensure that the results of the targeting process can be implemented. Thus task organization changes, modifications to the R&S plan, ATO nominations, changes to the HPTL and specified EFSTs all must be made with full awareness of time available to prepare and execute. While the time-focus for brigade targeting meetings is normally 24-36 hours out, certain targeting decisions, such as ATO nominations, must be planned for in conjunction with the theater or corps ATO cycle - which is usually based on a 72-hour cycle.

Preparation for the targeting meeting

4-58. A key to the successful conduct of the targeting meeting is preparation. Each representative must come to the meeting prepared to discuss available assets, capabilities, limitations, and battle damage assessment (if applicable) related to their BOS. This means participants must conduct detailed prior coordination and be prepared to provide the following inputs and/or information with them as described below.

4-59. The S3 section provides information on:

- Current friendly situation.
- Maneuver assets available.
- Current combat power.

- Requirements from higher headquarters (includes recent FRAGOs or taskings).
- Changes to commander's intent.
- Changes to task organization.
- Planned operations.

4-60. The S2 section provides information on:

- Evaluation of BDA.
- Current enemy situation.
- Current R&S plan.
- Planned enemy courses of action tailored to the time period discussed.
- Collection assets available and those that must be requested from higher.
- Proposed priority intelligence requirement (PIR).

4-61. The fire support section provides information on:

- HPTL, TSS, AGM or a consolidated matrix (for example., TSM).
- Fire support assets available.
- Proposed HPTL for the time period discussed and corresponding changes to FSCMs.
- Higher FS plan that affects unit operations.

4-62. Other staff sections provide information on:

- BOS asset availability and capabilities.
- The integration of their assets into targeting decisions.
- Capabilities and limitations of enemy assets within their BOS.

Conducting the targeting meeting

4-63. The XO (or S3) is responsible for keeping the meeting focused. He opens the targeting meeting by conducting a roll call, followed by a brief explanation of the purpose. He describes the agenda and specifies the time period to be addressed. He is the arbitrator for disagreements that arise (unless the commander is present) and constantly ensures allparticipantsare actively involved, staying on track with the stated purpose and agenda, and are not conducting *sidebar* discussions during the meeting.

4-64. Maximum participation by the staff is essential. Staff members and BOS representatives must share their expertise and respective staff estimate information on the capabilities and limitations of both friendly and enemy systems. They should also consider providing redundant means, if feasible, to detect, deliver and assess targets.

4-65. An example agenda for a brigade (informal) targeting meeting is:

- The S2 provides an intelligence update.

1. Briefs the enemy situation.

2. Reviews the current collection or R&S plans.

3. Provides battle damage assessment of targets engaged since the last targeting meeting and the impact on the enemy course of action.

4. Provides an analysis of the enemy's most probable courses of action and locations for the next 24-36 hours (possibly projecting out 72 hours for targets subject to attack through ATO nominations).

5. Recommends changes to the PIR for the commander's (if present) approval, or review by the battle staff.

- The S-3 provides a friendly situation update.

  1. Summarizes the current tactical situation; including new requirements.

  2. Informs on the status of available assets (combat power).

  3. If the commander is not present, briefs any particular guidance from the commander and changes to his intent.

  4. Briefs planned operations during the period covered by the targeting meeting.

- The FSCOORD or FSO provides an update on fire support.

  1. Reviews the current TSM (or other targeting products).

  2. Reviews status of FS assets.

  3. Reviews approved preplanned air requests for the period and those planned for the next two ATO cycles (this may be briefed by the ALO) - normally done in 24-hour increments.

  4. Presents a proposed HPTL with locations for the (commander's) staffs concurrence and refinement.

  5. Recommends ICW the ALO changes to the working preplanned air requests and nominations for the planning cycle.

- Once everyone understands what the enemy will most likely be doing for the next 24-36 hours, what the friendly plan is, and what targets have been recommended (approved if the commander is present) as HPT, the XO (or S3) completes the D3A process for those HPTs.

1. Decide and prioritize **what** detection assets are responsible for finding the target and triggering attack.

2. Decide **where** you will find the target, trigger its attack, and attack the target.

3. Decide **what** delivery means will be used to attack each target and the effects desired.

4. Decide **when** you will attack each target.

5. Decide and prioritize **what** detection assets will assess effects on the target, from where they will do so, and by when the information must be obtained.

6. Decide re-attack criteria and necessary actions.

- After all D^{3}A decisions have been made, **obtain the commander's approval**. Then prepare FRAGOs with new tasks to subordinate units and EFSTs. Rehearse if time permits. Begin (continue) tracking targeting actions by using the products your unit has adopted.

Appendix A

Examples of Fire Support Products

...RGET LIST (HIGH) PAYOFF TA...	
Priority	Target
1	Combat engineers (COBRA) on the main attack axis
2	TN1 and TN10
3	TN6, TN9, TN13

...ANCE MATRIX	...ATTACK GUID...	
Priority Targets: Attack within the security zone		
EFFECT	When	Remarks
...	...	...
TN1 and TN...	A	...
TN...	N/F	...

Timeliness	TPT	Accuracy
on the move	hologram	
ON 1 and 2S19	180m	

FIRE SUPPORT EXECUTION MATRIX - EXAMPLE 1

ATRIX - EXAMPLE 2 FIRE SUPPORT EXECUTION M

Appendix B

Artillery and Mortar Characteristics

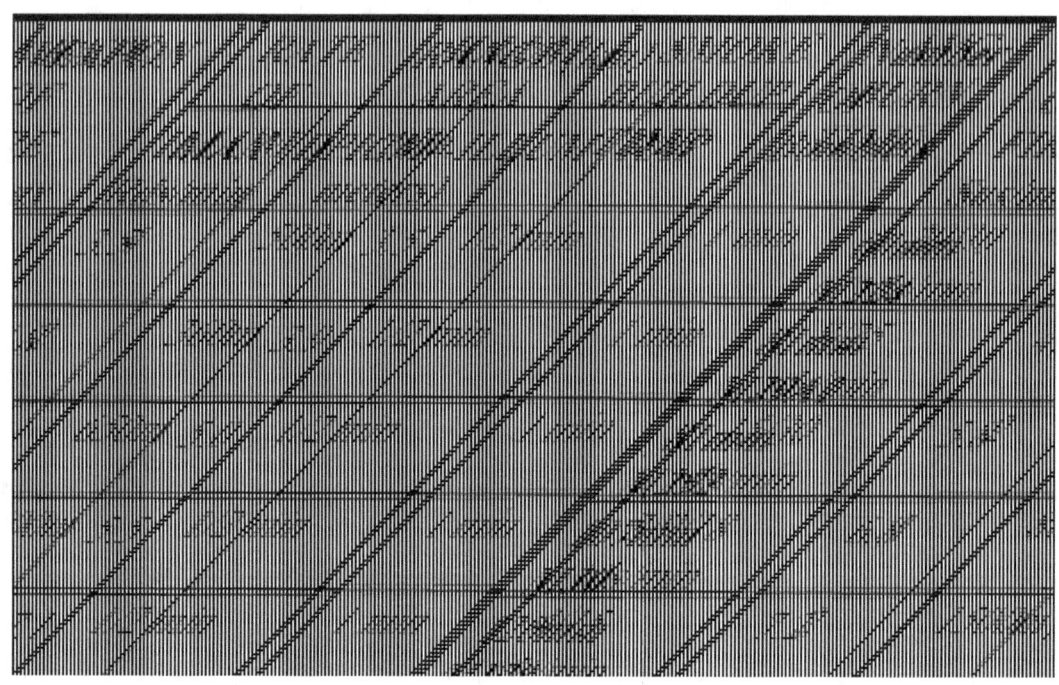

Appendix C

CAS Characteristics

Appendix D

Naval Surface Fire Support Characteristics

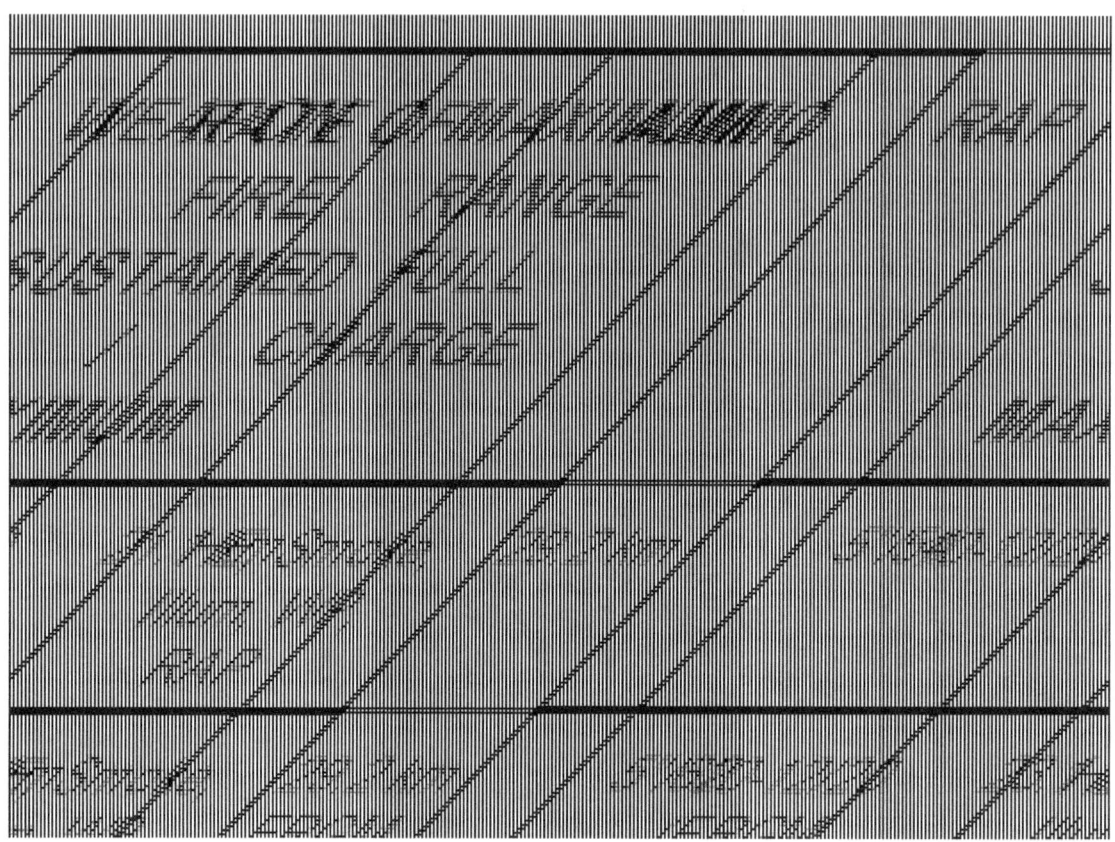

Appendix E

Target Acquisition and IEW Systems

Firefinder Radars

AN/TPQ-36

E-1. The AN/TPQ-36 is optimized to locate shorter-range, high-angle, lower velocity weapons such as mortars and shorter-range artillery. However, it can also locate longer-range artillery and rockets within its maximum range. For mortars and artillery, the higher probability of detection is approximately 12,000 meters. Minimum and maximum detection ranges can be established; however, at least 900 meters difference in maximum and minimum ranges is required.

E-2. The highly mobile AN/TPQ-36 is normally located **3 to 6 kilometers (km)** behind the forward line of own troops (FLOT). The AN/TPQ-36 can be emplaced and ready for operation within 15 minutes and can be march-ordered within 10 minutes for version VII systems during daylight hours.

E-3. The probability of location varies based on target type, range, quadrant elevation, and number of projectiles being simultaneously tracked. Other factors that may affect probability of location are target elevation above the mask, wind velocity, precipitation and the electromagnetic spectrum. In general, the Q-36 can locate at least five simultaneously firing weapons with quadrant elevations greater than 300 mils without degradation in location probability. This holds true as long as no more than two projectiles are being tracked or new firings do not occur at ranges greater than 7,500 meters from acquisition being processed. When both of these conditions occur, the probability of location may decrease by as much as 55 percent. Wind, rain and electromagnetic countermeasures do not degrade the performance of the radar when winds do not exceed 35 miles per hour, rain does not exceed 2 millimeters per hour or when a 100-watt ground based emitter's radiation is separated by five or more beam widths from the radar azimuth.

E-4. The probability of locating a mortar projectile is 90 percent or greater at ranges from 3,000-18,000 meters over the center 1,067mils of the radar's search zone. Outside the center zone the 90 percent location band is from 3,000-15,000 meters. For ranges from 750-3,000 meters the probability of location decreases from 90 to 45 percent in a linear fashion based on range.

E-5. The probability of locating cannons is 70 percent or greater for all ranges between 3,000 and 14,500 meters over the center 1,067 mils of the radar's search zone. Outside the center zone the 70 percent location band is from 3,000 to 11,500 meters.

E-6. Finally, the probability of locating rockets is at least 80 percent across the entire radar sector for all ranges from 8,000-24,000 meters. As previously discussed the target will be categorized as artillery. The range to the target and the results of IPB will likely be the only indicator that a target is a rocket.

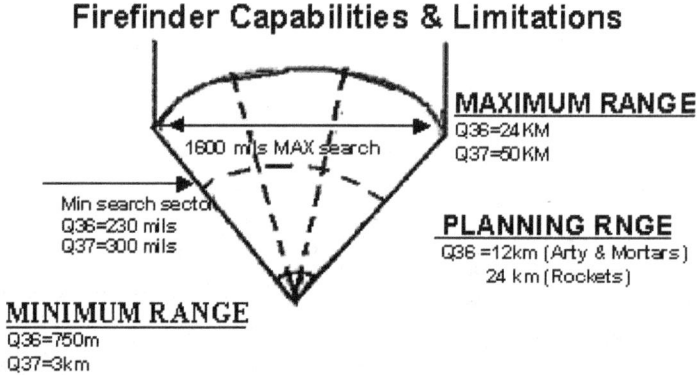

Firefinder Capabilities & Limitations

AN/TPQ-37

E-7. The AN/TPQ-37 is optimized to locate longer-range, low-angle, higher velocity weapons such as long-range artillery and rockets. However, it will also locate short-range, high-angle, lower velocity weapons complementing the AN/TPQ-36. For artillery, the higher probability of detection is approximately 30 kilometers. Minimum and maximum detection ranges can be established for the Q-37, but like those for the Q-36, at least 900 meters difference in maximum and minimum ranges is required.

E-8. The AN/TPQ-37 sector of search is from 300 mils minimum to 1,600 mils maximum. The Q-37 is normally deployed **8 to 12 km** behind the FLOT. The Q-37 can be emplaced and ready for operation within 30 minutes and march-ordered within 15 minutes during daylight hours.

E-9. The factors affecting the Q-37's probability of location are the same as for the Q-36. In general, the Q-37 can locate at least five simultaneously firing weapons with quadrant elevations greater than 300 mils without degradation in probability of location. This is true when no more that two projectiles are being tracked or new firings do not occur at ranges less than 6,000 meters or greater than three-quarters of the specified range for a specific projectile type. When both of these conditions occur, the probability of location may decrease to a probability of detection no lower than 50 percent. Wind and rain do not degrade the performance of the radar when winds do not exceed 40 miles per hour with gusts to 75 miles per hour and rain does not exceed 5 inches per hour with horizontal wind gusts of 40 miles per hour

E-10. The probability of locating a cannon projectile is 85 percent or greater at ranges from 4,000-30,000 meters when weapon quadrant elevations are greater than 200 mils at ranges less than 10,000 meters and 300 mils at ranges greater than 10,000 meters. The ranges vary depending on the size of the projectile. The range fan for detecting light cannon is from 4,000 to 20,000 meters over the entire search sector. For medium cannon, the range fan is from 4,000 to 25,000 meters over the center 1,067 mils of the search sector and 4,000 to 20,000 meters over the outside sector of the search sectors. The range fan for heavy cannon is from 4,000 to 30,000 over the center 1,067 mils of the search sector and 4,000-22,000 meter over the outside search sectors.

E-11. The probability of locating long-range rockets up to 762mm in diameter is at least 85 percent for quadrant elevations greater than 300 mils. The detection ranges are between 4,000 and 50,000 meters over the center 1,067 mils of the search sector and 4,000-37,000 meters across the outside search sectors.

Radar Zones Critical Friendly Zone

E-12. A CFZ is an area, usually a friendly unit or location, that the maneuver commander designates as critical. It is used to protect an asset whose loss would seriously jeopardize the mission. When the computer predicts that an enemy round will impact in a CFZ, the computer will report the location of the weapon that fired the round in precedence ahead of any other detection. Any location of a weapon firing into a CFZ will result in an immediate call for fire (FM;CFF message), unless it is manually overridden by the radar operator. The FM;CFF message is received by IFSAS/AFATDS as a Priority 1 message. Thus, a CFZ provides for the most responsive submission of targets to the fire support system. The CFZ is the only zone that does not have to be in the search fan of the radar. Some examples where the commander may use CFZs are: battle positions (BPs), passage points, breach points, air-assault/airborne LZs and PZs, forward scout positions, support by fire positions, attack by fire positions, choke points along maneuver routes, and aviation forward arming and refueling point (FARPs).

Call-For-Fire Zones

E-13. A CFFZ designates a search area forward of the FLOT that the maneuver commander wants suppressed, neutralized, or destroyed. An area designated as a CFFZ would likely be on enemy fire support positions and is closely tied to information developed during the IPB process and the HPTL. A CFFZ provides the second most responsive priority of request for fire generated by the radar. A target identified in a CFFZ will generate an FM;CFF Priority 2 message. However, the commander may upgrade this to a Priority 1 message for certain CFFZs. Some examples where a CFFZ may be used are: enemy mortar, artillery groups, and missile positions.

Artillery Target Intelligence Zones (ATIZ)

E-14. An ATIZ is an area in enemy territory that the maneuver commander wishes to monitor closely. Any weapons acquired in this zone will be reported to the IFSAS/AFATDS computer ahead of any other target detection except CFZ and CFFZ, but the detection will only result in a target report (ATI;CDR). Examples where an ATIZ could be used are the same as for a CFFZ.

Censor Zones

E-15. A CZ is an area from which the commander wishes to ignore any target detection. CZs must be used very judiciously, since the computer does not report to the operator a round originating from a CZ. A CZ may be used to ignore a friendly artillery position that, because of its aspect angle to the radar, could be detected as enemy artillery. This situation could occur when an uneven FLOT exists or when friendly units are in enemy territory. A CZ may also be used when artillery fires in support of rear operations.

Zone Management

E-16. Counterfire is not a separate battle and is the responsibility of the maneuver commander. Managing zones to facilitate the commander's intent and guidance is an important element in force protection and prioritizing fire support efforts. The keys to successful employment of radar zones are the interpretation of the maneuver commander's planning guidance and the integration of the fire support officers into the development, refinement and triggering of planned zones.

E-17. There is a distinct difference between zone management in the brigade sector, (AN/TPQ-36) and the division sector (AN/TPQ-37). In order to be responsive in the delivery of prioritized counterfire to support operations, such as breaching operations, the brigade combat team (BCT) and task force FSOs must be involved with the planning, refinement and triggering of the zones. Accordingly, the BDE FSE must prioritize the BCT sector and allocate radar zones to support the scheme of maneuver based on the commander's planning guidance. Critical to the success of the BCT's plan will be the coordination and availability of redundant radar coverage by the div arty (AN/TPQ-37). This coverage must be built into the planning guidance and coordinated as early as possible.

Striker/Reconnaissance (STRIKER)

E-18. The mission of the Striker platoon is to provide the maneuver brigade commander with dedicated observation teams that execute EFST throughout the brigade's AO. It is a dedicated asset that the brigade commander, through the brigade fire support officer, uses to execute EFSTs at depth for the brigade.

E-19. The Striker platoon leader acts as the FSO for the BRT. The platoon normally operates in direct support relationship to the brigade (whether formally or informally, vice operating in support of the BRT. Depending on METT-TC considerations, Strikers may be task organized to subordinate task forces. They operate out of the same or similar platform as the scout elements in the brigade and are capable of both dismounted and mounted operations. The Striker platoon can provide R&S as a secondary mission. However, execution of R&S tasks may impact its primary mission of providing the observation and subsequent attack of brigade HPTs and must be carefully balanced.

Combat Observation Lasing Team

E-20. The COLT is a brigade-level observer team designed to maximize the use of smart munitions. Although originally conceived to interface with the Copperhead munition, a COLT can be used with any munition that requires reflected energy for final ballistic guidance. COLTs can also be used as independent observers to weight key or vulnerable areas. The ground/vehicular laser locator designator (G/VLLD) provides the COLT with accurate range, azimuth and vertical angle to attack targets with standard munitions as well.

Improved Remotely Monitored Battlefield Sensor System (IREMBASS)

E-21. IREMBASS is a ground-based, all-weather, day and night, battlefield surveillance, target development, and early warning system capable of remote operations. Its purpose is to detect, classify and report in real time, personnel and vehicular (wheel and track) activities within the

area of deployment. The nominal sensor transmission range is 15 km, with an additional 15 km capability per employed repeater (part of the system).

E-22. Once in place, sensors can be left unattended for up to 30 days. The system will report a person, or tracked or wheeled vehicle to an operator station. The operator can use sensor data to calculate the number of targets, their location, speed and direction of travel.

Ground Surveillance Radar (GSR)

E-23. GSR teams provide mobile, all-weather battlefield surveillance. When employed in pairs they can provide observation from a given vantage point continuously. GSR targets are classified as dismounted, light vehicle, heavy vehicle, or tracked vehicle. The GSR has a line of sight range of 10 km against vehicles and 6 km against personnel. Though effective in low visibility, foliage, heavy rain and snow restrict its detection capability.

Other MI Company Assets

E-24. As the direct support organization for intelligence to the maneuver brigade, the DS MI Company provides enemy situational awareness data and target production. The company has counterintelligence and human intelligence (HUMINT) collection assets, UAV imagery capabilities and a common ground station (CGS) with which it can down-link broadcast intelligence including the Joint Surveillance Target Attack Radar System (JSTARS) feeds. When the MI company is task organized with non-lethal attack assets (EW) from higher, the FSCOORD and maneuver commander have additional options for the attack of high-payoff targets.

Glossary

A2C2	Army airspace command and control
ACA	airspace coordination area /air control party
ACE	analysis and control element
ACP	assault command post
ADA	air defense artillery
AFATDS	advanced field artillery tactical data system
AGM	attack guidance matrix/air to ground missile
ALO	air liaison officer
AM	amplitude modulated
AO	area of operations
AOC	air operations center
ATACMS	Army tactical missile system
ATIZ	artillery target intelligence zone
ATO	air tasking order
BCT	brigade combat team
BDA	battle damage assessment
BN	battalion
BOS	battlefield operating system
BP	battle position
BRT	brigade reconnaissance team
BSB	base support battalion
C2	command and control
CA	civil affairs

CAS	close air support
CBU	cluster bombs
CFFZ	call-for-fire zone
CFL	coordinated fire line
CFZ	critical friendly zone
CGS	common ground station
CLF	commander landing force
COA	course of action
COLT	combat observation/lasing team
COP	combat outpost
CP	command post
CPHD	Copperhead
CS	combat support
CSS	combat service support
D3A	decide, detect, deliver, and assess
div arty	division artillery
DPICM	dual-purpose improved conventional munitions
DS	direct support
DST	decision support template
EA	engagement area
EFAT	essential field artillery task
EFST	essential fire support tasks
ERGM	extended range guided munitions
FA	field artillery
FARP	forward arming and refueling point

FASCAM	family of scatterable mines
FASP	field artillery support plan
FBCB2	Force XXI Battle Command - Brigade and Below
FDO	fire direction officer
FFA	free fire area
FIST	fire support team
FLOT	forward line of own troops
FM	frequency modulation
FPF	final protective fire
FRAGO	fragmentary order
FS	fire support
FSCM	fire support coordinating measure
FSCOORD	fire support coordinator
FSEM	fire support execution matrix
FSO	fire support officer
GP	general purpose
GS	general support
GSR	general support reinforcing/ground surveillance radar
G/VLLD	ground vehicular laser locating device
HARM	high-speed anti-radiation missile
HC	hexachloroethane
HE	high explosive
HHB	headquarters and headquarters battery
HHC	headquarters and headquarters company
HIMARS	high mobility artillery rocket system

HPT	high-payoff target
HPTL	high-payoff target list
HQ	headquarters
hrs	hours
HUMINT	human intelligence
HVT	high-value target
HVTL	high-value target list
IAW	in accordance with
ICM	improved conventional munitions
IEW	intelligence and electronic warfare
IFSAS	initial fire support automation system
ILLUM	illumination
IO	information operations
IPB	intelligence preparation of the battlefield
IREMBASS	Improved Remotely Monitored Battlefield Sensor System
JAAT	joint air attack team
JSTARS	joint surveillance target attack radar system
km	kilometer
LANTIRN	low-altitude navigation and targeting infrared
LASM	land attack standard missile
LNO	liaison officer
LRSD	long-range surveillance detachment
LRSU	long-range surveillance unit
LZ	landing zone
m	meter

MBA	main battle area
MDMP	military decision making process
METT-TC	mission, enemy, terrain and weather, troops, time available, and civil considerations
MI	military intelligence
mins	minutes
MLRS	multiple launch rocket system
MOUT	military operations on urban terrain
MTC	movement to contact
NAI	named area of interest
NCA	National Command Authority
NCO	noncommissioned officer
NFA	no-fire area
O&I	operations and intelligence
OPCON	operational control
OPORD	operation order
PI	probability of incapacitation
PIR	priority intelligence requirement
PL	phase line
POF	priority of fires
PSYOP	psychological operations
PZ	pickup zone
R	reinforcing
RAG	regimental artillery group
RAP	rocket-assisted projectile

rds	rounds
recon	reconnaissance
RFA	restrictive fire area
RFL	restrictive fire line
ROE	rules of engagement
R&S	reconnaissance and surveillance
SASO	stability and support operations
SATCOM	satellite communications
SCATMINE	scatterable mine
SEAD	suppression of enemy air defense
SITTEMP	situation template
SLAM	supersonic low-altitude missile
SME	subject matter expert
SOI	signal operating instructions
SOP	standing operating procedures
SOSR	suppress, obscure, secure, and reduce
SP	self-propelled
TAC	tactical
TACP	tactical air control party
TAI	target area of interest
TF	task force
tgt	target
TOC	tactical operations center
TSM	targeting synchronization matrix
TSS	target selection standards

TTP	tactics, techniques, and procedures
UAV	unmanned aerial vehicle
UHF	ultra-high frequency
USAF	United States Air Force
USMC	United States Marine Corps
USN	United States Navy
VHF	very high frequency
WARNO	warning order
WP	white phosphorus
XO	executive officer

References

SOURCES USED

These are the sources quoted or paraphrased in this publication.

JOINT PUBLICATIONS

Joint Pub 1-02. *Department of Defense Dictionary of Military and Associated Terms,* 12 Apr 01

Joint Pub 3-16. *Joint Doctrine for Multinational Operations,* 5 Apr 00

ARMY PUBLICATIONS

FM 3-100.40. *Tactics*, 4 July 2000

FM 6-20. *Fire Support in the AirLand Battle*, 17 May 1988

FM 6-20-10. *Training Tactics and Procedures for the Targeting Process*, 8 May 1996

FM 6-20-40. *Tactics, Techniques, and Procedures for Fire Support for Brigade Operations (Heavy),* 05 Jan 1990

FM 100-5. *Operations.* 14 June 1993.

FM 100-6. *Information Operations.* 27 August 1996.

FM 100-7. *Decisive Force: The Army in TheaterOperations.* 31 May 1995.

FM 100-16. *Army Operational Support.* 31 May 1995.

FM 101-5. *Staff Organization and Operations*, 31 May 1997

FM 101-5-1. *Operational Terms and Graphics.* 30 September 1997

ALLIED PUBLICATIONS

STANAG 2437. *Allied Joint Operations Doctrine (AJP-1).* 15 December 1994.

STANAG 2928. *Land Forces Ammunition Interchangeability Catalogue in Wartime (AOP-6).* 9 June 1995.

STANAG 3680. *NATO Glossary of Terms and Definitions (AAP-6).* 3 October 1986.

DOCUMENTS NEEDED

These documents must be available to the intended users of this publication.

American-British-Canadian-Australian Handbook. December 1995.

JA422 *Operational Law Handbook, Judge Advocate General School.* 1994.

Joint Pub 3-16. *Joint Doctrine for Multinational Operations (draft).* 30 April 1996.

Joint Task Force Commander's Handbook for Peace Operations. 28 February 1995.

Presidential Decision Directive 25 (PPD 25). The Clinton Administration's Policy on Reforming Multilateral Peace Operations, May 1994.

STANAG 2101/QSTAG 533. *Establishing Liaison.* 28 June 1994.

Psychological operations studies that cover many countries around the world; may be obtained by writing to: Commander, 4th Psychological Operations Group (Airborne), ATTN: AORC-POG-SB, Fort Bragg, NC 28307-5240.

READINGS RECOMMENDED

These readings contain relevant supplemental information.

JOINT PUBLICATIONS

Joint Pub 0-2. *Unified Action Armed Forces.* 24 February 1995.

Joint Pub 3-0. *Doctrine for Joint Operations.* 1 February 1995.

Joint Pub 3-16. *Joint Doctrine for Multinational Operations (draft).* 30 April 1996.

Joint Pub 4-0. *Doctrine for Logistic Support of Joint Operations.* 27 January 1995.

Joint Pub 4-01.3. *Joint Tactics, Techniques and Procedures for Movement Control.* 21 June 1994.

ARMY PUBLICATIONS

AR 27-50. *Status of Forces Policies, Procedures, and Information.* 15 December 1989.

AR 34-1. *Rationalization, Standardization, and Interoperability Policy.* 15 February 1989.

AR 700-4. *Logistic Assistance Program.* 30 June 1995.

DA Pam 310-35. *Index of International Standardization Agreements.* 15 December 1978.

FM 55-10. *Movement Control in a Theater of Operations,* 8 December 1992.

FM 55-65. *Strategic Deployment,* 3 October 1995.

FM 100-23. *Peace Operations,* 30 December 1994.

ALLIED PUBLICATIONS

AAP-4. *NATO Standardization Agreements and Allied Publications,* December 1991.

STANAG 1149. *Doctrine for Amphibious Operations (ATP-8),* 21 December 1995.

STANAG 2014/QSTAG 506. *Operations Orders, Warning Orders, and Administrative/Logistics Orders.* 27 April 1994.

STANAG 2020/QSTAG 510. *Operational Situation Reports,* 14 July 1995.

STANAG 2103. *Reporting Nuclear Detonations Biological and Chemical Attacks, and Predicting and Warning of Associated Hazards and Hazard Areas (ATP-45),* 7 September 1995.

STANAG 2105. *NATO Table of Medical Equivalents (AMedP-1,* 21 September 1989.

STANAG 2394. *Land Force Combat Engineer Doctrine (ATP-52),* 12 January 1993.

STANAG 2406. *Land Forces Logistic Doctrine (ALP- 9[B]),* 29 May 1995.

STANAG 2868. *Land Force Tactical Doctrine (ATP- 35[A]),* 27 April 1992.

STANAG 2904. *Airmobile Operations (ATP-41),* 12 September 1985.

STANAG 2934. *Artillery Procedures (AartyP-1,* May 1994.

STANAG 2936. *Intelligence Doctrine (AintP-1[A]),* 16 May 1995.

STANAG 2999. *Use of Helicopters in Land Operations (ATP-49[A]),* 20 January 1994.

STANAG 3700. *NATO Tactical Air Doctrine (ATP-33[B]),* 27 July 1995.

STANAG 3805. *Doctrine for Airspace Control in Times of Crisis and War. (ATP-40[A]),* 9 March 1995.

STANAG 5621. *Standards for the Interoperability of NATO Land Combat and Combined Operations Systems,* 18 December 1989.

STANAG 6010. *Electronic Warfare in the Land Battle (ATP-51),* 12 February 1992.